What If and Why?

What If and Why?

Literacy Invitations for Multilingual Classrooms

Katie Van Sluys

Heinemann
Portsmouth, NH

Heinemann
A division of Reed Elsevier Inc.
361 Hanover Street
Portsmouth, NH 03801–3912
www.heinemann.com

Offices and agents throughout the world

The author and publisher wish to thank those who have generously given permission to reprint borrowed material:

"Come with Me" by Naomi Shihab Nye. Copyright © 2000 by Naomi Shihab Nye. Published by Greenwillow Books. Used by permission of HarperCollins Publishers.

Library of Congress Cataloging-in-Publication Data
Van Sluys, Katie.
   What if and why? : literacy invitations for multilingual classrooms / Katie Van Sluys.
      p.   cm.
   Includes bibliographical references and index.
   ISBN 0-325-00732-2 (alk. paper)
   1. Language arts.   2. Group work in education.   3. Education, Bilingual.   I. Title.
LB1576.V335 2005
372.6—dc22   2005012514

Editor: Kate Montgomery
Production service: Denise Botelho
Production coordinator: Vicki Kasabian
Cover design: Jenny Jensen Greenleaf
Typesetter: Kim Arney Mulcahy
Manufacturing: Louise Richardson

Printed in the United States of America on acid-free paper
09 08 07 06 05 RRD 1 2 3 4 5

For my teachers in learning and life—
especially Nancy, Rise, Jerri, and all the
children and teachers I've met . . .

Contents

Invitations

Acknowledgments

"We learn from the company we keep . . ." (Smith 1998, 30). This quote captures the essence of my experiences as student, teacher, researcher, colleague, and author. It posits that the authoring of this book is not an individual accomplishment but the collective work of those with whom I've had the good fortune of working with over the years.

My first note of thanks goes to the children, teachers, and school community I had the pleasure of working with while in Indiana. Children of all ages constantly pushed my thinking about possible images of what literacy learning is and ought to be. Their teachers' careful attention to their students' every move inspired me to keep writing so that we could invite others to engage in conversations and actions aimed at rethinking the world. The school's principal, teachers, and staffs' understandings of curriculum, kids, and the demands of teaching helped grow a community of educators who were not just dialoguing about change but engaging in the everyday job of rethinking literacy learning contexts and opportunities for *all* students—within classroom and beyond. This school community constantly reminded me that, yes, change *is* possible.

From writing conferences and suggested readings, to check in phone calls and pictures that capture students at work, this book would not have come together without Dorothy Menosky, Carolyn Burke, Rise Reinier, Amy Seely Flint, Tasha Laman, Mitzi Lewison, and Anne DeFelice, colleagues who continually push my thinking. I also am indebted to all that Heinemann has given me and this book. Kate Montgomery and Alan Huisman are a writer's dream—their attentiveness to process, their encouragement, and their dedication to seeing a project through is admirable. From the first day I met Kate, I knew that working together would be an extraordinary pleasure. She is an educator, advocate, and coach dedicated to enriching the lives of children and bettering the world through writing that connects with the educational community. Her enthusiasm and constant, thoughtful feedback inspired me to put into words the exquisite teaching and learning I was part of during my Indiana University years.

I wrote this book in my new Chicago home. Nearby friends and new colleagues in the city also contributed to this work. Kelly O'Connor, graduate assistant extraordinaire read drafts, gathered resources, made suggestions, and edited throughout the process. The elementary school across the street welcomed me with patience as I moved between writing and getting to know their school community. Friends attended to the on-the-go dimensions of my writing process as they ran with me along the lakeshore, listened to my ideas over dinner and coffee, or took me away from the computer when I needed it. Friends and family living at a distance understood my focus, encouraged my progress, and reminded me why I teach and how this writing is teaching.

Introduction

Come with Me

> Come with me
> To the quiet minute between two noisy minutes
> It's always waiting ready to welcome us
> Tucked under the wing of the day
> I'll be there
> Where will you be?

> —*Naomi Shihab Nye*

Naomi Shihab Nye—poet, listener, writer, musician, activist, advocate for unheard voices, and deeply caring human being—has long been an inspiration to me. Nye's poem "Come with Me" invites readers into a time and place away from the busyness and noisy chatter of everyday living. The words suggest a need for a space where people can come together to pause, reflect, think, and take action in light of new understanding. They resonated with sixth-grade Sara and her experiences emigrating from Northern Africa to the United States. Sara copied Nye's poem into her writing notebook and carried it with her, then entered English-speaking worlds through her own poetry that conveyed the challenges of immigration, learning English, and making friends.

I offer this book as a place to step back from our day-to-day classroom activity to take stock of where we are in terms of language and literacy learning, reflect on the opportunities offered to all students, and consider where we might go from here. I invite you to "come with me" and explore the notion of curricular invitations as one option for involving English language learners in important conversations and actions that move beyond learning language to using language, communicating, and acting in ways that contribute to creating a better world.

What Does It Mean to Be Literate?

We know that children enter schools with vastly different experiences: some have traveled extensively; some have nontraditional families; some are avid newspaper readers, or soccer players, or dancers, or TV watchers, or cartoonists; some are in between countries and cultures; some are familiar with a wide array of new technologies; some have navigated issues connected with race, class, gender, or social or political concerns; some communicate in languages other than English. Given the wide range of students' experiences and educational contexts, efforts to celebrate diversity surface in some school conversations and appear on some agendas while remaining buried in others. Educational research encourages teachers to reconsider the roles of students' out-of-school knowledge (Moll 2001), cultural and linguistic resources (Thomson 2001; Gutierrez et al. 1999), and social worlds (Dyson 1999) in curriculum. At the same time, politicians prescribe educational mandates under the guises of raising standards, holding schools accountable, and giving all students equal opportunities to learn. As we enter the twenty-first century, we need to reexamine how literacy is taught and used in our schools. As teachers of both mono- and multilingual students, we need to reexamine what it means to be literate. We need to consider how definitions and decisions privilege some students and disadvantage others. We need to understand our options, clearly articulate our perspectives, and take action both in our classrooms and in the wider world.

Issues related to literacy learning, cultural and linguistic diversity, and social action have weighed on my mind since I entered the teaching profession as a hopeful young educator. On my second day of teaching, my principal, as one way of addressing the changing linguistic landscape of our school and community, created a bilingual kindergarten and I became its teacher. As I came to know students, families, and my own teaching, I tried to live my commitment to positioning students and their various ways of knowing at the center of curriculum while attempting to add previously unheard voices to conversations about school policy. Our classroom was filled with multilingual texts; invited language learners to use Spanish, English, art, music, drama, and play to construct meaning; and included the perspectives of parents and other wider-community members. In my efforts to take these perspectives beyond the classroom, I joined district committees addressing issues of cultural and linguistic diversity with hopes of diversifying committee membership and viewpoints. I wanted to be part of making our schools welcoming and engaging for all learners.

In the years that followed, as I taught in multiage and international settings, I continued to question the sorts of literacy practices offered for both new and more experienced English language learners. Moving back to the United States after teaching for two years in Mexico, I was fortunate to spend four years investigating literacy and language issues with preservice and practicing teachers, elementary students, and university colleagues. We wondered how children's cultural lives could truly be honored in everyday classroom curriculum; questioned how students' first languages could be positioned as valuable tools in their learning; explored how instructional or programmatic structures influence the sorts of literacy practices in which multilingual students are invited to participate; and investigated what students see literacy learning and school as being about and for. This line of thinking fed my commitment to studying how particular practices influence students' literate futures and who they become, and this book grows from and furthers these efforts.

I see writing this book as a form of social action. Believing that all learning is social, I draw on the voices of students, colleagues, friends, and family to articulate and share what I think it means to be literate and, given our increasingly broad understanding of literacy, how we can reimagine some of the literacy practices in our classrooms. I want to invite classroom teachers, ESL/ELL/ENL teachers, preservice teachers, administrators, and teacher educators to think and talk about language learning, language learners, and the social implications of literacy instruction.

Contributing Perspectives

Several key experiences and perspectives have shaped the thinking in this book.

First, it is grounded in a holistic, critical perspective toward literacy learning. My ongoing interactions with colleagues like Rise Reinier, Kevin Gallagher, Mitzi Lewison, Amy Seely Flint, Jerome Harste, Dorothy Menosky, and Tasha Laman have played a large role in shaping my thinking about the social dimensions of becoming literate. A critical perspective pushes us to think about becoming literate in ways that move beyond decoding or encoding printed words or mastering a "standard" grammar to thinking about how language is used to accomplish social ends. It moves us beyond students' merely learning language to students' becoming critical users and consumers of language as a means of taking action in their world.

Second, I believe that we learn language, learn through language, and learn about language as we engage in meaningful endeavors with others (Halliday 1978). From this perspective, language learning is a cognitive, transactive process of prediction and confirmation in which language learners use their knowledge of patterns, social contexts, and meaning-making conventions to construct meaning as well as communicate with others. Schools are social worlds that may or may not share the same norms or practices as other communities of which the students are members (Heath 1983; Hicks 2002; Au 2001; Michaels 1985; Wheeler and Swords 2004, Christenbury 2000). Student experiences may vary as to mode of communication, goals, pattern of interaction, and/or first language. While students for whom English is not their first language and/or who come to school knowing and speaking "non-Standard" varieties of English may differ on the surface from their "Standard" English-speaking classmates, they share deep structural similarities as language learners. We know that new English language learners use first-language acquisition strategies (Collier 2004) and that all language learners search for linguistic and cultural patterns appropriate to the communities in which they find themselves. I therefore invite you to join me in considering curricular perspectives and structures that allow all students to become proactive users of language rather than passive recipients of language instruction.

Last, in enacting this perspective toward literacy in everyday classroom practice, I build on Carolyn Burke's concept of "invitations," first introduced in a graduate seminar in 1981. Burke's invitations have the following characteristics:

1. The learning environment is social and collaborative.
2. The focus is on making meaning.
3. The invitation is open to users with varied knowledge, varied experience, and varied language flexibility.
4. The invitation accurately reflects the best current understanding of any alternate knowledge system used.
5. The invitation is open to alternate responses.
6. The invitation is a single focused engagement, not a series of exercises or activities.
7. There is potential for further inquiry.

Invitations move beyond celebrations of diversity (heroes, holidays, food fairs, and cultural days/months) to become real inquiries that are centered around students' lives, invite critique, and encourage transformational thinking and social change. In this book, you'll find definitions and explanations of what invitations and critical literacy are all about, checklists to help you set up your classroom, suggested resources, example invitations, and classroom vignettes illustrating how the perspectives we take toward literacy matter as well as where and how we might begin to engage students in hopeful curriculum.

Choosing Our Terms

The words we use convey particular perspectives and reflect different worldviews. Therefore I need to explain the terms I use related to language use and language users. The children that have contributed so much to my thinking were students at a public elementary school and included both participants in an English as a new language (ENL) program and native English speakers. To me, all these children are English language learners (ELL). Daily life and their interactions with one another call them to learn language, learn about language, and learn through language (Halliday 1978).

In describing students for whom English is not their home language, I've decided to use the language of the school the students attended; I believe these terms honor the students' knowledge and experience. The term *English as a new language* (ENL) refers to immigrant and/or U.S.–born students whose home language is not English and who receive English language learning support in addition to interactions with their classroom teacher and peers. There are bi- or trilingual students who do not require this support. In the school in which I worked (and specifically within the intermediate classroom I refer to as Room 4), ENL teachers often worked with students in their regular classroom, side by side with the classroom teacher. As opposed to *English as a second language* (ESL), ENL also recognizes the many students who are learning English as a third or in some cases fourth language. Perhaps most important, ENL reflects a perspective toward learning language that is not angled toward "English only."

You're Invited

I hope our journey together offers hopeful images of what is possible as well as suggests paths that can be taken in classrooms near and far to create better worlds for all language learners—beginning with the young people in your classroom.

What If and Why?

What Are Invitations?

When we hear the word *invitations,* we probably think about being asked to attend parties, celebrations, meetings, or other social events. We might also think about the decisions we make when we receive an invitation. Will we accept it? Who else will be there? What will our responsibilities be? Do we know what happens at a baby shower? a birthday party? a holiday celebration? And even if we've attended a particular kind of event before and know what to expect, each opportunity has a unique context and different guests with different interests and cultural expectations.

Invitations solicit people to come together to engage in an activity of mutual interest. Those in attendance collaborate with others, valuing their perspectives and ways of being. The activity is contingent on purpose, theme, those who gather, participant experiences, questions raised, and available resources. And once one joins a given gathering or activity, there are often more than one option for how to participate.

In educational contexts, invitations may bring to mind classrooms in which students choose among a wide variety of activities (Routman 1991). However, the term *curricular invitations,* as used in this book, means something different. Curricular invitations have properties that are similar to social invitations to join committees, work as a member of a task force, attend celebrations, or participate in civic activities.

The Invitation to Vote

To explore what is and isn't meant by the concept of invitations in this book, let's look at a familiar social invitation—voting. In a democracy, citizens who meet certain criteria (eighteen years of age or older and in good standing) are invited to vote. People aren't required to vote; they are presented with voting as a social opportunity. Accepting the invitation does not result in the same actions or activity for each voter.

Imagine three different voters: an eighteen-year-old; a longtime member of the Democratic Party; and a thirty-year-old voting for the first time. Chris has just turned eighteen and talks at length about candidates with his grandmother as they sort through the campaign materials she receives in the mail and discuss the ads he's seen on the Internet. Despite their long talks, when Election Day arrives Chris decides not to cast formal votes because he still isn't sure he knows which candidates to choose. Angelica, who has voted in every election since her eighteenth birthday, is an active Democrat and has campaigned for the party's local candidates. She goes to the polls knowing exactly how she will cast her votes. Kim, a first-time homeowner appalled by his property taxes, decides that this year he will make it to the polls. He is certain about which city candidates to vote for based on their positions on taxes, but is much less sure about the state and national candidates. Waiting for his turn to vote, Kim talks with other voters in line, and they wonder about the truth behind campaign promises and theorize about what might happen if property taxes continue to rise. When Kim walks into the booth, he confidently casts his city votes and makes best guesses for the rest.

Chris, Angelica, and Kim have each taken up the formal invitation to vote in his or her own way. Their preparation is based on different experiences. Their decisions about how or whether they will participate and whom they will vote for vary. Regardless of these differences, their experiences are similar in two ways: all three are using language to learn about voting processes and gather needed information, and all three (whether they know it or not) are gaining new insights about language itself.

Curricular Invitations

Invitations in the classroom, like the voting invitation, also have two layers. There are formally crafted invitations, or pieces of curriculum (like the laws that invite those eighteen and older to register and subsequently vote), that contain many smaller but authentic component opportunities for participants to inquire, interact, and learn (as Kim, Angelica, and Chris searched the Internet, talked with friends and family members, participated in party-affiliated meetings, chatted informally with fellow voters at the polls, or consulted the media). Formal, "umbrella" invitations state a purpose or focus for an inquiry or investigation (whether short term or large scale) and provide or suggest tools with which to initiate and organize the activity. Component invitations are the various ways participants use language and other ways of knowing to learn within the context of the larger inquiries. In both social and curricular invitations, participants are decision makers from the start. They decide which invitations to pursue, with whom, and how.

While this book is mostly about formal curricular invitations, it is anchored in the understanding that students are language users, not language recipients. As students learn *through* language, they learn language. What they learn about language and the kind of language they learn (language of retelling, language of mathematics, language of critique, etc.) depend on the activity. Furthermore, participants' surroundings and understandings of available and possible practices is key to all learning—including invitations.

To paint a clearer image of curricular invitations in classrooms, let me begin with what they are not. Invitations are not centers. They are not scripted activities in which everyone must follow the same route or address identical questions. They are not assigned research projects or inquiries that must result in written reports. They are not geared to a predetermined response or a single answer.

According to Mitch, a member of the Room 4 community, invitations are about "educational choice." His classmate Anthony adds that "what makes invitations educational is that you learn new things that you never knew before." Continuing to listen in on a conversation between Mitch, Anthony, and their classmate Trevor as they prepare a presentation about invitations paints an even richer image:

TREVOR: With invitations, there are people helping you.

MITCH: Collaborating with you, reading with you—

TREVOR: Writing, making posters, drawing, making music—

ANTHONY: Researching, getting ideas, thinking about what's on their minds.

MITCH: There's the folder that guides you, it's like an outline because invitations can take so many different directions. It depends on the people—

TREVOR: And the questions people ask and what people are trying to do.

ANTHONY: Even if you've already done an invitation a million times you can still go back again and learn completely new things. Questions and invitations just go on and on and never end.

These boys make it clear that invitations are built on the understanding that all learning is social. Their conversation refers to how learners are invited to work together to pursue focused inquiries related to themes and issues that matter to them. Zooming in even further, let's look at a vignette of a curricular invitation in action.

It's the Friday before spring break. Sixth grader Steve leans across the table and asks his fourth-grade classmate Emily, "What are you going to do for invitations when we get back?" The sign-up board across the room lists some of their choices:

- *If the World Were a Village*
- Images of Mexico
- *Seedfolks*
- Maps
- Hair
- Memories

Without waiting for Emily to answer, Steve excitedly announces, "I'm doing a new one about money—it's not up there yet."

Earlier that week Steve had shared his interest in currency from around the world. He lived in England as a young child and knows about the pound. After subsequent conversations with classmates and teachers, he has begun to put together a collection of world currency. Examining some of the coins one morning he noticed that money from England, Canada, Belize, and Hong

Kong all depicted the queen of England. "Why is the queen on all of these coins?" he wondered. His teachers asked him, "Would you like to learn more about that? You could do that during invitations." He immediately answered an energetic yes—enthusiasm that has apparently stayed with him as he shares his upcoming plans with Emily. (The currency invitation his teacher created is shown below.)

When Steve finishes telling his plans, Emily explains that she too is thinking about creating an invitation of her own. She has been reading *Coolies* (Yin 2003) and talking with her grandfather about their ancestors who helped build the transcontinental railroad. She has been looking at the format of two other invitations—one about homelessness and one on Paul Fleishman's book *Seedfolks* (1999)—in which roles are designated for readers to take on as they explore various related texts. "I'm thinking about setting it up like those," she says.

In the days and weeks after spring break, Steve, Trevor, Andréa, and a number of other students pursue invitations under the currency invitation umbrella. Using Steve's initial collection of currency from around the world plus additional examples contributed by other class members (Andréa brings

---

INVITATION: Exploring Currency

Just before spring break Steve was looking at his currency collection and wondered, "Why is the queen of England on all these coins?"

You're invited to explore as many examples of world currency as you can. If you like, use a hand lens to help you take a closer look.

What do you notice about the money?

Are the coins and/or paper currency related in any way(s)? If so, how can the relationships be explained?

What questions come to mind?

Resources

Books

Currency (Inventions That Shaped the World series) by Patrick K. Kummer

Money by Margaret C. Hall

Empire of Mali by Carol Thompson

Websites

Currency converter: www.x-rates.com/calculator.html

American Currency Exhibit: www.frbsf.org/currency/

The Euro: http://europa.eu.int/euro/entry.html

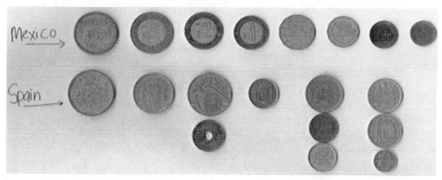

FIGURE 1–1. Currency graph

in coins from Brazil; Sara, from Algeria), the students begin to research connections between England and countries whose currency refers to British royalty. They begin to question their understanding of "the colonies" (the thirteen colonies that became what is now the United States of America) and the broader notion of colonization. But their inquiries don't stop here. One week, Sara and Steve bring a balance over to the table where they are working and weigh the coins as they talk. Sara draws on her knowledge of Arabic and French as she explains what is written on the Algerian dinar paper currency, and she tells Steve about her first encounters with U.S. dollars. Another week, Gino and company graph the currency by shape, size, and country (see Figure 1–1). And when Trevor and Steve use Google to search the Internet for currency calculators to determine exchange rates, Nina suggests adding plus signs (+) between the words *coins, exchange,* and *calculator.* Locating a useful site, they plug in numbers and click on calculate. Then Trevor wonders how they could figure out exchange values without the computer calculator, and Steve wonders, "Why doesn't one penny equal one peso? Who decides how much each one is worth?"

Properties of Critical Invitations
Invitations have properties that distinguish them from centers or teacher-directed activities. The ones detailed here are based on the original invitations designed by Carolyn Burke and my collaborations with Mitzi Lewison, Amy Seely Flint, Jerome Harste, Dorothy Menosky, Rise Reinier, and the inhabitants of Room 4. These properties guide how invitations are created as well as suggest how to construct the environment in which they occur and the ways in which we might observe and think about those who undertake them. Critical invitations:

1. Occur in social learning environments.
2. Focus on making meaning around one experience.
3. Welcome varied experiences, languages, and resources.

4. Represent our best current understandings.
5. Embrace opportunities to use multiple ways of knowing to construct and contest meaning.
6. Value alternative responses.
7. Promote the social aspects of learning by taking up issues in students' lives and placing inquiries within social contexts.
8. Encourage practices that reach across all dimensions of critical literacy.
9. Invite further inquiry.

Seven of these nine properties are closely tied to Carolyn Burke's early work with invitations (see the Introduction); properties 7 and 8 are new, and Chapter 2 discusses them in detail.

It is not always easy to carve definitive lines within the properties of invitations. However, using the currency invitation as an example, let's examine how these properties play out in the classroom. As we consider each property, keep in mind that intersections and overlaps are common.

Invitations Occur in Social Learning Environments

The company, thinking, and perspectives of others make the learning in the currency invitation social. As Steve gathers his initial collection of currency, talks about his early experiences living in England, and chats with Emily, his learning involves others. In the weeks working on the currency invitation, Emily, Steve, Sara, Trevor, Andréa, Gino, and the rest continue to learn together. However, learning from and with others doesn't always require physical presence. Learning as social endeavor means that one's thinking is informed by all preceding interactions with people, texts, and lived experiences. For example, as Steve and Trevor are sitting at the computer investigating exchange rates, Steve turns to Trevor and wonders how much Andréa's December trip to visit relatives in Brazil really cost. Andréa isn't working with the boys, but her previous contribution has prompted a new question.

Invitations Focus on Making Meaning around One Experience

Steve's interests, questions, and wondering are the source of the teacher-created formal invitation. As different groups of participants join in, they generate informal invitations (exploring the physical properties of the money; comparing and contrasting coins by size, weight, and value; questioning colonization) that zoom in on an area of specific interest while still being related to the broader notion of currency.

Invitations Welcome Varied Experiences, Languages, and Resources

Invitations are for everyone. They are not extras, extensions, or remedial experiences. They are open inquiries that invite all learners to enter with what they know and use their resources in the course of their work. Consider the range of what transpires from Steve's initiating interests and questions.

Andréa's immigration experiences added to Steve's experiences introduce new dimensions and possibilities. As students examine the fine print on various forms of currency, they turn to classmates who speak that language. When they begin to explore exchange rates, Trevor's mathematical understanding is a key resource. When they search the Internet, Nina's technological skills help them locate useful resources.

The range of experiences, languages, and resources in classrooms is wide. While not every invitation needs to fit every student, we must pay attention to the range of students in our classrooms and allow for people of varied experiences to work together. When groupings encompass diverse experiences, students teach one another in ways that not only extend one another's understanding of the world but position diverse student experiences as valuable, useful learning tools. The definition of what it means to be a successful, literate student also shifts.

Invitations Represent Our Best Current Understandings

If we examine why and how we learn in our own lives, we find that it's often the complex and difficult issues that invite intense thinking and sustained attention. While at times we might yearn for simple answers, complex problems are rarely paired with simple solutions. They require contemplation, hypotheses, proposed solutions, successes, and failures.

We have to be careful not to break down scenarios, questions, or wondering into potentially uninteresting parts. For example, Steve and his classmates are not limited in what they can investigate or what they find. As they imagine how many pesos one might need to make a dollar, they wonder how much money people make in Mexico. With each discovery comes new complex questions. Had they been confined to identifying, comparing, or contrasting the weight of various coins, notions of world economies might not have surfaced.

Also, their work doesn't answer all their questions. At times their questions, interests, and inquiries require more information, as when they wonder who decides exchange rates and locate Internet resources that explain trade, exchange rates, and global economies. As they read articles line by line they work together to understand ideas and bring bigger questions to the class when they share their work. Their work reminds us that we need not simplify the world for children or divert them from complicated issues that engage them. This experience does not make these students sophisticated economists, but the questions they ask and investigate alter not only their previous notions and experience of how the world *is* but who they are as literate people: critical inquirers who use language to *question* how the world is.

Invitations Embrace Opportunities to Use Multiple Ways
of Knowing to Construct and Contest Meaning

Invitations embrace opportunities to use multiple ways of knowing (language, dance, drama, art, music, mathematics, gesture, etc.). While decoding and encoding words and communicating mathematical ideas using symbols ($2 + 4 = 6$) are probably most familiar to us, opening up communicative possibilities that reach beyond reading, writing, and speaking creates new possible points of entry for learners as well as new possible destinations.

Communicating and making meaning are group processes. Meaning isn't fixed; rather, it is constructed by people interacting in particular cultural settings. We share the meaning of symbols like letters, pictures, artifacts, numbers, characters, visual images, and so forth through our interactions and shared experiences. Take the relationship between the value and size of United States coins: size doesn't have a direct, consistent correspondence with value. We know this because of our experiences with quarters, dimes, nickels, and pennies. This relationship is cultural, however, not absolute: the size and value of pesos *do* correspond. The symbols are similar but the hypotheses one may form are anchored in culturally constructed understanding. Equally important, the currency artifacts impact who and how participants join in the activity. Sara and Steve frequently manipulate the pieces of currency and use them as props. Reading Arabic becomes a valued way of knowing, as do mathematics and symbolic communication (graphing, sorting, etc.).

If we rely on language alone, we place unnatural limits on learning. In everyday life, certain meanings are better communicated in song, painted image, or diagram than in words alone. We draw on more than one way of knowing when we say we're mad, cross our arms, and distance ourselves from the group or write a reflective entry in a journal. Encouraging ways of knowing other than language alone—creating spaces where learners can bring their scientific, economic, geographic, or historical knowledge to bear on the task at hand—adds to the kinds of meaning that are created and questioned.

When classmates Andréa and Steve "read" the pictures of the queen printed on the currency, they construct significantly different meanings. Steve's limited understanding of colonialism similarly limits his hypotheses. Andréa, however, draws on her knowledge of Brazilian history and Brazil's initial connection with Portugal, suggesting that the countries that depict the queen's picture on their currency might have been connected at one time and wondering whether they still are. Technological knowledge is used when Nina stops by the computer at which Steve and Trevor are working. The boys have entered *coins* and *calculator* into an Internet search engine in an effort to figure out exchange rates and aren't getting anywhere. Nina suggests adding the word *exchange* and demonstrates how to use the + sign in a Google search. After this search directs them to a useful site, Nina returns to her work, and Steve and Trevor continue their inquiries.

These students don't merely discover new insights in various media; they use multiple ways of knowing as they come to new understanding. They don't just see one another as "experts" known for specific talents or skills; rather, they use their diverse knowledge to question others' thinking, to push inquiries further, and to become integral members of their classroom literacy community.

Invitations Value Alternative Responses

Invitations are a time for inquiring, making meaning, and questioning. They are not about producing a research paper, doing a required drawing, and so forth. Student responses are contingent on their questions and the paths they follow in answering them. Therefore, there is no expected response, no desired outcome, and no definitive ending. Visions change as participants interact. If an invitation produces a poster, graph, map, or piece of writing, it is a by-product, not the "result." Invitations allow participants to dig into complex issues; they often find themselves in places they never meant to be as they learn from the tensions and confusions that surround them and/or ask new questions.

Take the currency graph: it is not a static product but a tool for thinking. An experienced mathematician might not consider it very refined, a teacher might have specific graphing criteria on her mind, but these things aren't what matter in this instance. The graph is created in the course of thinking; it is both a pictorial response to questions and a prompter of new questions (about raw materials, minting processes, and who decides what words and images appear on money).

Invitations push us to put aside our need for tangible products, to trust that learners' activities are or will be purposeful, and to realize that process is as important as product, if not more so.

Invitations Promote the Social Aspects of Learning by Taking Up Issues in Students' Lives and Placing Inquiries Within Social Contexts

Invitations ask students to investigate real issues in their everyday lives. Steve is initially interested and intrigued by the diversity of currency. Given time to explore the samples he's collected, he makes observations that lead to questions. His teachers closely attend to his questions and concerns and use them as the basis for a formal invitation. The initiating questions, the invitation design, the accessible resources, and the students' related experiences take them beyond the personal (living in England, collecting coins, etc.) to the surrounding social contexts and issues (fluctuating exchange rates, unequal economies, colonialism past and present, etc.).

Invitations Encourage Practices That Reach Across All Dimensions of Critical Literacy

Critical literacy is social: disrupting the status quo, questioning, studying taken-for-granted assumptions, acting for change. It is reading the world and taking action. While participating in invitations may foster students' growth as artists, mathematicians, linguists, engineers, musicians, writers, it also creates space for growing as democratic and/or literate citizens who critically reflect on their world and work to change it. But critical practices don't just happen. They're acquired through experiences.

A "four-dimensions" framework (Lewison, Flint, and Van Sluys 2002) pulls together the breadth of thinking about critical literacy and has helped educators think about what critical literacy in action looks like in the classroom. This framework, which is explored in Chapter 2, can be used to examine the sorts of activities students are engaged in, as well as offer opportunities that encourage taking on new practices.

Invitations Invite Further Inquiry

Invitations are far from finite. When initial questions are open-ended and authentic, there are no simple solutions. Studying real issues always leads to new questions. It is not enough to report that one peso isn't equal to one dollar, that plus signs between key words in Internet searches are helpful, or that Panama uses the U.S. dollar as its dominant currency. Rather, when we make discoveries, encounter contradictions, or experience tensions, we begin new inquiries. Steve's initial questions prompt several lines of inquiry that other students pursue from many angles even after Steve moves on to other invitations.

Continued inquiry takes on a range of meaning—it may involve asking new questions, gathering more information, and/or suggesting a course for future action (redesigning currency to reflect racial diversity or political autonomy). Continued inquiry may also mean leaving a topic and applying newly acquired ways of seeing, thinking, or questioning to the next learning endeavor. It may alter the ways readers read or respond to future texts. It may mean questioning something on a billboard, in a magazine, or in a TV commercial. Invitations engage participants in real work that requires living as an inquirer and developing critical ways of being.

How This Book Is Organized

Now that you have an idea of what an invitation looks, sounds, and feels like, we're ready to move on. Chapter 2 looks more closely at literacy perspectives that will help you design and implement invitations in your classroom. It focuses on how to define and look at student actions in light of these perspectives. Chapter 3 walks you through how you might set up a classroom that encourages the kind of work Steve, Emily, and their classmates engage in. It also addresses how to design invitations for your teaching contexts. Chapters 4 and 5 dive into how you can discover issues on your students' minds, craft related invitations, and match materials to the issues that matter most in students' lives. Chapters 6 and 7 explore potential teaching practices to encourage deep reflection and refinement of literacy practices as students learn to live as active invitees. And Chapter 8 offers tools to help document journeys, make teaching decisions, see what students are doing as well as who they are becoming. At the end of each chapter, "Invitations for All" invites you to look up from the pages of this book and reflect, try out, plan, and take action to make critical invitations a reality in your students' lives.

Reflecting on Language as a Living Process with Many Options
Steve raised an initiating question that resulted in the creation of the currency invitation, which led participants in many related directions. When you think about how invitations are framed and created, keep in mind that there are always other options. How else might you frame Steve's initial question as an invitation?

Here are two options that come to my mind. Many of the same component invitations may be triggered by these new options. Then again, these new options may lead participants down completely different paths.

"It All Comes Down to Money."

What does it mean when people say something like that? You're invited to explore examples of foreign currency and consider possible meanings connected with this phrase.

Look closely at the words and images printed on money. What do you notice? What you can find out? What do the words and images say about the country? To what ideas are the words and images connected? Who decides what is printed on money?

How Much Does It Cost?

You want to travel or move to another country, but before deciding where, you need to know how much it might cost. You're invited to think about places you might like to go and investigate potential costs.

Find out what currency is used in a place you'd like to go. What do you need to know about currency exchange in order to figure out what it might cost to move to or visit this place? What happens when you (or other people) convert one country's currency into another? How might exchanging currencies affect your (or other people's) lives?

2

Joining the Critical Literacy Club

What is literacy about and for? Thinking specifically about literacy and schooling Barbara Comber (2001) writes, if children "only knew about literacy from being in school, what would [they] think it was for?" (100). Fifth grader Alissa would place taking action for social change at the top of her list of possible responses to such questions—it is how she lives her life. Take the day she walked back into her classroom after noon recess and began writing furiously in her notebook (see Figure 2–1). When she'd finished, she brought her concerns and frustrations to a class meeting.

Her classmates then added their perspectives, concurring with and challenging Alissa's stance. Some cited other exclusionary playground practices; others mentioned how well their class had played soccer together earlier that year. They suggested that games like soccer were inclusive activities that transcended language diversity because everyone did not require the same language experiences in order to play them.

Adam, Trevor, and Nina referred to their work together on a technology invitation for which they'd prepared a PowerPoint presentation on noon-hour football. They supported Alissa's position on football's gender bias. Hearing Nina's perspective was particularly significant. As a student new to English, Nina was often hesitant to speak in large groups. However, she was known for her technological literacy and often made her thoughts public through technological tools (prerecorded voice tracks, the words and images of various computer software programs).

The class' conversation then expanded to include the gender lines that permeate professional sports and the job market in general. In the days that followed their discussion of Alissa's writing, Alissa, her classmates, and their teacher submitted essays and political cartoons to their class newspaper on gender, equity, and access to sporting events. Earl, who happened to be drafting a list of rules for noon-hour football, made a significant revision based on his classmates' feedback. His writing is included in Figure 2–2.

These students were using literacy not only to make issues visible but to elicit the perspectives of others and to organize for social change: to make a difference. They were encouraged to address issues of local and global concern as well as position their personal issues within larger social contexts,

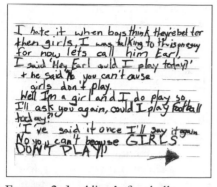

FIGURE 2–1. Alissa's football writing

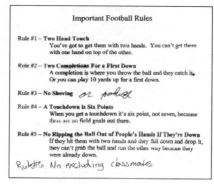

FIGURE 2–2. Earl's writing

connecting Alissa's experiences with larger cultural story lines involving sports, gender roles, and social change. Together their literacy practices valued multiple ways of knowing, as they made their thinking known through writing, talk, technology, and drawing. Through their work they explored an array of perspectives. Tackling a playground issue, they participated passionately in an activity that contributed to their understanding of what literacy is about and for—as well as who they were in their literate community. They learned whether they were valued members, if their real questions mattered, and if school could be a place to explore what was really on their minds. They learned whether they (boy, girl, shy student, bold person, English-dominant learner, ENL student, Caucasian, Korean, immigrant, adopted child, American-born child) could or couldn't succeed in their classroom.

Becoming Critically Literate

Becoming literate means joining a literacy club (Smith 2002) in which we see ourselves as valued, credible members. As we construct our definitions of what it means to be a member of the critical literacy club and, in particular, an invitations participant, it is helpful to connect our beliefs with those of current literacy theorists.

Invitations are anchored in a critical perspective recognizing that becoming literate is about becoming a particular kind of person. Life is complicated and requires more than knowing how to read words, spell conventionally, or converse fluently in a given language. Therefore, taking a critical perspective toward learning language and becoming literate involve orchestrating diverse linguistic and cultural resources in order to engage in literate activity that:

- explores relationships between language and people;
- considers diversity and difference as essential;

- includes agency, reflection, participation, and action; and
- proceeds from the premise that we can't guarantee the problems and dilemmas students will encounter in their future lives.

Curriculum is thus geared to helping us become problem posers who authentically study our complex and complicated social lives (Friere 1972; Harste 2001; Short, Harste, and Burke 1988).

Critical literacy involves knowing about our social world and knowing how to critique it (Green 2001), as Alissa did when she brought football inequities to the curricular table. Critical literacy includes knowing how to take action and design new options for making the world better, as Earl did with his proposed rules. Being critically literate involves questioning how texts work ideologically (Luke and Freebody 1997), listening to and evaluating competing voices (Harste as cited in Edelsky 1999), and acting in ways that can transform social conditions (Friere and Macedo 1998). Linda Christensen (1999) reminds us that becoming critically literate is also about engaging in academically rigorous work that is grounded in students' lives, always connected to larger contexts, and based on the hopeful premise that students can create the world in which they want to live.

Critical literacy practices are as diverse and varied as the contexts in which they occur. Moving from definitions into the classroom, we can begin to think about practices that invite questioning. Whose voices are heard? Whose are left out? Who is marginalized in particular situations? Who makes decisions? Who benefits and who suffers?

For example, a class investigating the social issues in David Smith's *If the World Were a Village* (2002) might assemble Unifix-cube trains to represent the distribution of Chinese, English, Hindi, Spanish, Arabic, Bengali, Portuguese, and Russian speakers worldwide and in so doing question why English is the dominant language of commerce or why Serbian languages aren't even mentioned when they are the dominant languages of some students' neighborhoods.

Critical practices question group and power relationships. They take up issues of how gender, race, class, and families are represented and explore the taken-for-granted (Bomer and Bomer 2001). Critical practices move beyond notions of common sense to cultural sense, addressing how and why we come to construct what seems *natural* in the world. Such practices envision literate people as those who question "how things get done" (Comber 2001) or expose who is neglected in society and then work for justice.

As part of critical literacy, students and teachers also explore how texts work ideologically, how they attempt to position readers in particular ways. For example, imagine a newspaper article about failing schools. The article begins on the front page underneath the headline "Maplewood Elementary and Nine Other Schools Failing," includes a photograph of two students from Maplewood, and discusses how these ten schools have been labeled as failing based on their students' standardized test scores. It contains quotes from politicians and administrators as well as numeric reports of annual yearly progress (AYP). How might a group of students read this text critically?

They might wonder why only one school was named. They might notice that although students are pictured, their voices are not part of the story. They might bring to bear their knowledge of the learning taking place in their own school: "I don't see how they could say this about Maplewood—from the beginning of the year a lot of people have come a long way with learning language. And I don't think that it should be based on testing, there's so much more. You need to be here to know." These critically conscious consumers might investigate the complex ways in which language learning takes place during the year and address the ways in which students new to English as a language of instruction participate in the curriculum. They might decide to find out more about school districting, community socioeconomics, and the distribution of linguistically diverse students within the school population.

Reading this article critically means looking at what is present in the article as well as what is missing. It includes paying attention to how words, images, and visual design are used to convey *particular* meanings. It includes recognizing the role of power in telling a story and outlining future action.

Recent work in critical literacy offers powerful possibilities for constructing readers and (re)designers of worlds (Friere and Macedo 1998; Medina 2004). Second graders in Tim O'Keefe's classroom investigate social justice in written conversations with their family members (Jennings with O'Keefe 2002). Young students in Vivian Vasquez's (2000) classroom lobby for the right to participate in school activities from which they are excluded. Jane Hammel's (2003) students explore how poverty is dealt with in the picture books they read, while students in Rise Reinier and Kevin Gallagher's (2003) class use their class meeting to get involved in current events. Students in Lee Heffernan's (2003; Heffernan and Lewison 2003) room redesign morning meeting, write social narratives about their own experiences, and create new possibilities for action.

I have watched firsthand as two teacher researchers helped their students become critically literate. Anne DeFelice's first, second, and third graders wondered about the relative position of girls and boys in the presidential fitness program and exposed differences in standards by collecting articles, taking notes, and constructing graphs. Heather Caudill's students explored what is meant by power and prompted her to question her own practices as an active teacher researcher.

Because critical literacy can play out in so many ways, we need tools to help us think about how to introduce critical practices in our own classrooms. One possible tool is the four dimensions framework (see Figure 2–3), which Mitzi Lewison, Amy Seely Flint, and I developed (Lewison, Flint, and Van Sluys 2002). The framework pulls together four dimensions of critical literacy practice: disrupting the commonplace, considering multiple viewpoints, focusing on the sociopolitical, and taking action.

Disrupting the Commonplace	*Considering Multiple Viewpoints*
Critical literacy is about seeing the "everyday" through different lenses. We have the responsibility to choose and use diverse lenses to examine how we use language and other sign systems to interrogate "how it is" and to consider other ways to understand experience.	Another dimension of critical literacy describes multiple viewpoints asking us to imagine standing in the shoes of others while relating others' perspectives to our own.
• Problematizing all subjects of study and understanding existing knowledge as a historical product (Shor 1987);	• Reflecting on multiple and contradictory perspectives (Lewison, Leland, and Harste 2000; Nieto 1999);
• Interrogating texts by asking questions such as "How is this text trying to position me?" (Luke and Freebody, 1997);	• Using multiple voices to interrogate texts by asking questions such as "Whose voices are heard and whose are missing?" (Luke and Freebody 1997);
• Including popular culture and media as a regular part of the curriculum for purposes of pleasure and for analyzing how individuals and groups are positioned and constructed by television, video games, comics, toys, etc. (Marsh 2000; Shannon 1995; Vasquez 2000);	• Paying attention to and seeking out the voices of those who have been silenced or marginalized (Harste et al. 2000);
• Developing the language of critique and hope (for achieving social justice) (Shannon 1995); and	• Examining competing narratives and writing counter-narratives to dominant discourses (Farrell 1998); and
• Studying language to analyze how it shapes identity, constructs cultural discourses, and supports or disrupts the status quo (Fairclough 1989; Gee 1990).	• Making difference visible (Harste et al. 2000).

FIGURE 2–3. Four dimensions framework

Focusing on the Sociopolitical

Everything we do is political. Paying attention to the ways in which everyday politics, sociopolitical systems, power relationships, and language are intertwined and inseparable from teaching and learning is central to this dimension of critical practice.

- Going beyond the personal and attempting to understand the sociopolitical systems to which we belong (Boozer, Maras, and Brummett 1999);
- Challenging the unquestioned legitimacy of unequal power relationships (Anderson and Irvine 1993) by studying the relationship between language and power (Fairclough 1989; Gee 1990);
- Using literacy to engage in the politics of daily life (Lankshear and McLaren 1993); and
- Redefining literacy as a form of cultural citizenship and politics that increases opportunities for subordinate groups to participate in society—literacy is an ongoing act of consciousness and resistance (Giroux 1993).

Taking Action

Becoming critically literate involves taking informed action. By engaging in practices associated with the other three dimensions, practices within this dimension involve using literacy to achieve social justice.

- Engaging in *Praxis*—reflection and action upon the world in order to transform it (Freire, 1972);
- Using language to exercise power to enhance everyday life and to question practices of privilege and injustice (Comber 2001);
- Being an actor versus a spectator (Freire 1972);
- Continuing analysis and study of how language is used to maintain domination, how nondominant groups can gain access to dominant forms of language without devaluing their own language and culture, how diverse forms of language can be used as cultural resources, and how social action can change existing discourses (Janks 2000); and
- Challenging and redefining cultural borders, encouraging students to be border crossers in order to understand others, and creating borderlands with diverse cultural resources (Giroux 1993).

Source: Lewison, Flint, and Van Sluys (2002)

FIGURE 2–3. *Continued*

An Invitation in Action

In order to invite our students to become critically literate people, we must have a way of looking at what they're doing, identifying points of departure and starting points, and creating images of what critical practices might look and sound like. To better understand the four dimensions framework, let's look at it in the context of an invitation in which two young ENL students investigate the racial images of motherhood in Mother's Day ads. Their teacher had noticed her students' reactions to advertisements in the daily newspaper and the Scholastic catalogue. She had also recently read Jennifer O'Brien's (2001) piece about studying language using Australian Mother's Day sales brochures. Combining her observations and O'Brien's thinking, this teacher created a Mother's Day–Ads invitation designed to encourage critical study. The text of the invitation was stapled to the outside of a folder containing an array of recent newspaper ads.

The two girls working on this invitation, Fernanda and Nokomo, are both new to the English language, and to the United States, within the last year. Fernanda's first language is Spanish; Nokomo's, Russian and Mongolian. During their year in Room 4 they have already used literacy practices in connection with other invitations and are aware of available resources. As you read about the girls' activities, pay particular attention to the ways in

---

INVITATION: Mother's Day Ads

Lately class members have noticed newspaper ads as well as the fine print in book order leaflets. They have noted what ads include and exclude.

You're invited to examine some of the recent ads related to Mother's Day that are included in this folder.

You might choose to consider some of the following questions as you read and think with other invitation participants.

- What do you notice?
- What questions come to mind?
- What do you notice about gender?
- What do the ads tell you about celebrating Mother's Day?
- How does the organization of the ads contribute to meanings?
- Who benefits from these messages?
- What options do you have as a reader of these texts?
- How might you respond?

Resources
Mother's Day ads from newspapers, magazines, store circulars

which their work focuses on social conditioning, how their lives are part of their learning, and how they use diverse ways of knowing.

One Wednesday morning in mid-May, Fernanda and Nokomo sit side by side looking at a picture of three young, thin, Caucasian women in a discount store's Mother's Day ad.

"These not moms, they models or university students," Nokomo declares, then moves to a neighboring table and rummages through a pile of newspaper ads looking for an image she considers to be motherlike. Locating an ad featuring larger women, she shows Fernanda the picture: "These moms."

"Not mine," replies Fernanda, and their inquiry begins.

Nokomo has assumed that Fernanda shares her perspective that not all mothers are thin, but Fernanda is thinking along a different line. Speaking quietly in short phrases, Fernanda uses pictures and dramatic gestures to make her point: "Not white."

The girls then begin looking through the pile of ads together and cannot find any images of African American, Latina, or biracial moms. Nokomo says, "No Mongolians," referring to her own heritage, and then adds, "This America."

Who are Americans? Does being American mean being white? As they continue working, Nokomo shares her prediction that "one hundred percent of America is white minus a little percent." Wondering about the racial makeup of the U.S. population, they go over to a library computer and "ask Jeeves."

Fernanda types, "How many Americans black and white?" in the text box, but Nokomo suggests entering only "black and white." The sites produced are associated with black-and-white photography. "White" produces sites associated with the white pages of telephone books. Switching to the Spanish version of the search engine, Fernanda types in "población de los Estados Unidos." When I suggest using the limiting term *race* in conjunction with their previous search the girls find the information they need.

According to the 2000 census, 12 percent of the United States population is African American, 75 percent is white, 12 percent is Hispanic or Latino, and 1 percent is of Asian descent. Noting that nearly a quarter of the population is nonwhite, the girls wonder why the women in the ads are mostly white. Shouldn't one-quarter of the ads look like one-quarter of Americans?

Fernanda and Nokomo print out the population statistics and create a poster to share with their classmates. They tape the original ad in the center of a large piece of paper, attach the statistics they discovered on their Internet search, and add some of their own thoughts. Then they show their poster to Kelly, who, with three other classmates, has also worked with Mother's Day ads. Glancing at their poster, Kelly says, "We did this too, but we did it different"—reminding us that an invitation can be approached in many ways, depending on the participants, their experiences, and the questions currently on their minds.

Fernanda and Nokomo finally present their poster and their evolving thinking to the class, and the students have an animated discussion about stereotyping moms: *What about mothers and sons? What about kids that don't have moms? What about moms that want to go to college? What about the stuff that isn't in the ads, like tools, camping gear, or electronics?* Their comments call into question the dominant notion of American mothers being propagated by the American retail industry. Their collective talk invites additional perspectives, connects their small-group experiences with the larger world, and changes the way they read the Mother's Day advertisements.

Imagine what Nokomo and Fernanda might have learned about literacy and their lives if the literacy practices in their classroom focused on reading grade-level stories and completing corresponding response activities like surveying classmates about places they would like to visit, listing what they like and dislike about the illustrations, or sequencing the story's events. Would they see their lives and experiences as relevant? Or would they see literacy as making lists, sequencing events, or following predetermined agendas? Would they learn to question and take action or to live in the world as is?

Mapping Critical Practices Using the Four Dimensions

How can Fernanda and Nokomo's work be understood in terms of critical literacy? What makes it critical?

Globally, their work is concerned with issues of representation—predominately gender and race. Academic rigor, which according to Christensen (1999) is integral to effective critical pedagogy, is present as these students use and refine their research skills to critique dominant cultural models. They question the *taken-for-granted* or *natural* as they ask, "Why is it like this?" They question how the texts are operating in the world (Luke and Freebody 1997) by exposing the stereotypes being perpetuated. They also talk with their classmates about how redesigning these texts could transform current social conditions (Green 2001).

Analyzing Fernanda and Nokomo's activities in terms of the four dimensions framework—disrupting the commonplace, considering multiple viewpoints, focusing on the sociopolitical, and taking action—let's us see what they were and were not yet doing in this invitation.

Disrupting the Commonplace

Critical literacy is seeing the "everyday" differently. We are responsible for choosing diverse lenses to examine how we use language and other sign systems to question "how it is" and for considering other ways to understand experience. Practices associated with this dimension might include asking:

- How has history shaped our understanding of _____?
- What are the underlying messages?
- What language is being used? Does the language used support or disrupt the status quo? How is it positioning the reader?

- What are the authors' intentions?
- What texts are we reading to understand the world (books, comics, video games, the Internet)?
- What tools do we have for critiquing how it is and imagining how it could be?
- What other sources can we consult to further explore _____?

Nokomo and Fernanda's work with the Mother's Day ads grows from their everyday lives—the advertisements they see and the things they experience as immigrant students. The girls first read "against the grain": their opening statements that the women featured in the ad are "not moms." As they work together questioning "how it is," they use their working definitions of reading—pointing to pictures, speaking phrases, manipulating technological tools, and drawing on both English and Spanish.

Considering Multiple Viewpoints
Another dimension of critical literacy describes multiple viewpoints, asking us to imagine standing in the place of others while relating others' perspectives to our own. Practices associated with this dimension might include asking:

- Who wrote this? Why?
- Whose voices are heard and whose are missing?
- What are the authors telling us? What are they leaving out?
- Who can we turn to in order to learn more about other perspectives?
- How else could the story be told?
- How do the various viewpoints differ? Do we consider particular perspectives "normal"? If so, why?

Remember Fernanda's initial response to the images Nokomo thinks are more reflective of mothers? Nokomo is thinking only about body image. Fernanda introduces race as another factor. With this perspective on the table, the girls know where to turn to gather census information about what images will fairly reflect the racial composition of the United States.

Focusing on the Sociopolitical
Everything we do is political (reading from a scripted lesson, choosing to read or not read particular books, closing our classroom door, joining a protest, ignoring or taking up playground conflicts, etc.). Paying attention to the ways in which everyday politics, sociopolitical systems, power relationships, and language are intertwined and inseparable from teaching and learning is central to this dimension of critical practice. Practices associated with this dimension might include asking:

- How are our personal experiences related to larger cultural stories, systems, or experiences?
- Who has power? Why?

- How are language and design used to achieve or maintain power?
- What other readings or meanings are possible? What about the world would need to be changed to make other readings plausible?

The girls' work with the Mother's Day ads is closely tied to stories of what it means to be American with regard to race, class, and gender. Their collaborative research on the computer initiates questions about the power of advertisers to ignore and/or erase nondominant images. Their talk with classmates initiates cultural story lines centering on "what mothers would like"—jewelry, kitchen appliances, clothing—as well as what products are missing in the ads—sporting gear, books, electronics, leisure-time items. They also question the emphasis on material goods—what about moms who just would appreciate time to relax and families who can't buy the items in the ads? Power is ascribed to these images, and their collective work questions assumptions that could be overlooked in a more passive reading.

Taking Action

Becoming critically literate involves not only reading words and worlds (Friere and Macedo 1998) but also taking informed action for change. As we live critically, we need to take what we have learned from our critical readings and strive for social justice. Doing so might involve asking:

- In what ways are participants interacting and talking back to texts as they interact with authors and/or text designers?
- In what ways do critical practices invite reflection about ourselves and our own actions in the world?
- Do practices include analyzing the role of language in domination? What language or languages are used (social languages; dialects; Spanish, Arabic, English, Korean)? Not used? What would happen if the languages drawn on and used changed?
- Do participants actively take on new positions in an attempt to understand others?
- In what ways is language used to question, rewrite, and resist privilege and injustice?

Fernanda and Nokomo work together. Taking action begins as they talk back to the advertisements in front of them and continues as they generate and propose alternatives about what moms like (see Figure 2–4) and make a poster that shares their findings with the class. Presenting their thinking using spoken and written language in conjunction with visual images, they raise questions and facilitate a discussion: *what about children that do not have moms? what about moms that do things not pictured in the ads?* They have a social agenda. As a group they recognize that even if some mothers might like jewelry, other moms might prefer other things that show appreciation or help them learn and grow as people. Action here encompasses reading resistantly, communicating new lines of thinking, and pushing others to question how they come to see the world.

A Vision of What Is Possible

In the Mother's Day–Ads vignette, Fernanda and Nokomo make use of their *lived experiences, diverse resources,* and *understanding of critical literacies.* Fernanda reads the advertisements as a Latina girl and notices the absence of Latina women. Nokomo echoes the dominant idea of what it is to be American when she notes that Mongolians are absent because "this [is] America." Their inquiry is also propelled by their previous experiences with invitations. They read beneath and behind what appears "normal" within everyday social issues. They know where newspapers are kept in their classroom and understand the importance of gathering additional information to inform their thinking. Thinking, rather than a single language, is what matters. When their English language searches fall short, Fernanda shifts to the Spanish version of Internet Explorer. And as they gather useful findings, they use visual images from the ads, tables printed off the Internet, their own writing, and talk to convey their thinking.

FIGURE 2–4. Fernanda and Nokomo's list of things moms like that are absent from ads

When we aim for literacy practices that move beyond merely reading the words on the page, that go on to question how words and possible meanings are linked to the surrounding world, we need options. Critical curricular invitations are one means of engaging students in socially relevant investigations as they work in a number of languages and draw on a wide range of cultural resources and tools for making meaning. Take a moment to look closely at your students and what they think literacy means.

INVITATIONS FOR ALL

Reflecting on Language as a Social Process in Your Classroom

Fernanda and Nokomo were attracted to Mother's Day Ads. What other kind of text might appeal to your students—a short newspaper article, a photograph, an informational letter about a school policy, a picture book addressing a social issue relevant to their lives? Invite them to read and respond to it. Watch them. Take notes. Invite them to draw or write in response to their reading and/or discussion. Collect any artifacts they produce.

Take a closer look at your students' work and their current understanding of literacy using the four dimensions framework. Can you locate questions, statements, or reflections that disrupt the commonplace? Are there times when students elicit or mention other viewpoints? Do they refer to larger social contexts? Are there places where action can be taken?

Use what you notice and learn about and from your students. Can you locate a beginning point for you and them? Venturing into critical literacy isn't an overnight trip; it's a long journey that calls for students (and those of us who work with them) to change our perspective about what literacy is and how it should be used.

Setting Up Invitations

3

Creating supportive conditions and practices for curricular invitations is like getting ready for a party. We need to decide where the party will be held, the things we'll serve, what we'll do when. While these decisions are important, a great location, fabulous food, and exciting activities alone don't guarantee a successful gathering. Success also hinges on what the guests know about the event as well as party etiquette. For example, experienced partygoers heading to an open house, where guests are expected to come and go, might arrive midway through the designated hours. However, when invited to an awards dinner, they would try to be prompt.

Just as successful parties call for thoughtful preparation and guests who understand expectations, the same can be said about planning for and engaging in curricular experiences and other school-related events. For example, we wouldn't take our students on a field trip without carefully thinking through the purpose for the excursion and the logistical details. Nor would we host extracurricular activities without shared visions for agendas, activities, and responsibilities. Rather, we would plan, make sure our students had the necessary background experiences, and discuss our expectations with our students. Setting up invitations in our classrooms calls for similar planning, preparation, and shared vision.

If we want students to raise and pursue questions that are important to them and the world (*Why does the value of money change? Who decides that girls can't play recess games or certain sports? Why are most of the women in Mother's Day ads white?*), they need a supportive learning environment in which they are encouraged to ask about and respond to critical issues. They need to know that we (as an inquiry community) value their voices, welcome their perspectives, and recognize that inquiring into critical issues is complex work that won't always lead to quick and easy answers.

To create environments that successfully support invitations, we need to think through procedural, environmental, and practice-oriented considerations in our classrooms. Specifically, we need to:

- Make time for invitations.
- Create productive workspaces.
- Organize invitations and related materials.

25

- Design written invitations that honor the requisite properties.
- Give students choices about which invitations to pursue.
- Establish sign-up procedures.
- Make invitations interesting and engaging.
- Build in opportunities for reflection.
- Allow students to share their thinking, experiences, insights, and processes.

Making Time for Invitations

One of our first questions when considering new curricular opportunities is, where can we find the time in already busy school days? The answer involves more than finding a few extra minutes or hours, it entails making curricular decisions. We first need to think about what literacy learning is about and for and connect that with what takes place during an invitation. In working through an invitation, students read, write, think, compose, and challenge meanings. They communicate with others, pose problems, formulate questions, explore possible responses and/or solutions, as well as organize new inquiries. When these sorts of actions are important curricular outcomes, invitations are an integral tool for supporting student growth.

Making time for invitations might mean rethinking divisions between science and literacy lessons; it might mean creating invitations that deal with conflicts highlighted in social studies; it might mean highlighting mathematical problem solving within particular invitations. Bottom line, it requires believing that the processes students engage in during invitations will help them develop as literate people.

For an invitation to be successful, there needs to be enough time for sustained inquiry. In my experience with both primary and intermediate students, blocks of time ranging from forty-five minutes to two hours are appropriate, depending on the students' familiarity with the concept and the process. As with reading or writing workshops, students ease gradually into longer blocks of time as they learn to take responsibility for their learning. As they come to see that they won't be constantly interrupted, that they're not seeking simplistic answers or racing to be done, they will begin to dig into the complexities of the issues they're thinking about.

While a regular schedule is helpful, we must be careful not to isolate or separate invitations from the overall work of the classroom. They aren't stand-alone activities but relate to larger agendas, interests, and ways of being in the classroom. Questioning norms, exploring multiple viewpoints, studying the politics of living, and taking action should become regular practices that reach beyond students' work with formal invitations.

Creating Productive Workspaces

Conducting inquiries in conjunction with others requires spaces in which small groups can gather, spread out materials, and work without interruption. Classrooms these days are usually cozy places with a number of discrete areas, and we can use these smaller spaces to great advantage. We can:

- Try to create several places in which kids can collaborate without working on top of one another.
- Request tables instead of desks, or arrange the desks into clusters.
- Use bookcases, carpets, file cabinets, or carts to help divide space into distinct areas.
- Configure clusters of computers around the periphery of the room so that they are accessible to as many groups as possible.
- Consider space outside the classroom. Is it possible to use the hallway? Is there a corner of the library we can sign up for at the same time each week? Can teacher aides or parent volunteers supervise a group or two in another room?

Once we have a number of potential workspaces, we can match them with our groups' sizes and needs. Groups working on an invitation that requires computer software or Internet access can do so in the computer center, groups that need floor space to spread out their work can meet on the rug by the reading chair, and so on. We can identify and label workspaces by name (*rug, table 5, book nook*) and list the name of the space along with the invitation on the sign-up board. Or we can place each invitation in the location we want students to work on it. We need to be flexible and open to student suggestions and our observations regarding what works best for our classroom.

A productive environment involves more than its physical arrangement. Invitation participants also need tools and materials that will support them as they think, explore, and work with others. It's not possible to anticipate what path a particular invitation will take, so students need to be able to find what it is they decide they need. For example, one of the properties of invitations is that making meaning and communicating are accomplished through many ways of knowing in addition to written and spoken words. Students could be reading, writing, talking, researching, painting, sculpting, building, taking things apart, dramatizing, playing instruments, listening to music, exploring works of art, using technology, and more. However, because participants should be the ones to decide how they want to construct and communicate meaning, we can't just include clay, paints, or a tape recorder with a given invitation. When planning classroom layout, procedures, and norms, we should ask:

- Are artistic tools like paints, markers, paper, instruments, scissors, etc., available as needed?
- Can students research the Web, listen to audiotapes, or watch segments of movies or films?
- Are microscopes, balances, math manipulatives, tape recorders, etc., easily available and used as part of everyday learning?

- Are classroom libraries organized so that students can find resources quickly?
- Can students go to the media center, library, computer lab, and similar school locations? Are there policies and procedures whereby they can make phone calls to local libraries or area experts?

Making these conditions a reality in our classroom might mean creating an art center, setting up computer stations, reorganizing the classroom library, or providing a "Where are you working?"/"What do you need?" message board.

Whatever systems are in place or created, it is important that they aren't teacher dependent. We want students to make their own decisions and carry on their work independently. That way, rather than attending to procedural and material needs, we can work with or observe specific groups of learners.

Organizing Invitations

A convenient way to organize invitations is in two-pocket folders. In Room 4, the "invitation"—the written document that initially outlines and focuses the activity—is often stapled on the outside of the folder. Inside are related newspaper articles, brochures, calendars, product labels, picture books, excerpts from novels or nonfiction books, poems, maps, diagrams, and so on, along with work produced by the students who have already worked on the invitation. The invitation on pages 29–30 illustrates how an invitation to explore gender roles might be set up.

The folders can then be stored in a drawer, tub, or other location that students can get to easily if they want to do additional work or consult a book or resource before the next formally scheduled invitation workshop. If we want students to undertake meaningful inquiries over time, we must be careful that invitations are always accessible and not artificially relegated to certain periods of the day.

Also, there may be times when more than one group is working on the same invitation. In that case, we can make additional copies of the cover sheet and set up several folders. However, the resources in each folder need not be exactly the same. For example, if there was a great deal of interest in the gender roles invitation, we could spread the resources over three folders, each of which offers slightly different possibilities for approaching the investigation.

Designing Written Invitations

In previous chapters, we've discovered the properties of invitations, looked at one or two examples, and listened in as invitations have played out in the classroom. To help make invitations a reality in our classroom, let's look at how written invitations are crafted to allow learners to focus their activity, make decisions that will make the invitation relevant to the particular group, and encourage inquiry into local and global social issues.

Written invitations have a common architecture. When we receive a party invitation in the mail, we expect to be told the time, date, and place in

INVITATION: Exploring Gender Roles

On the Outside of the Folder

Authors write stories that convey characters, plots, settings, and conflicts through words and illustrations. Readers pay attention to what's happening in the story. Critical readers also look at what stories say about the world.

You're invited to explore texts of your choosing. Some are included with this invitation; however, also feel free to explore the classroom library, books or magazines you're currently reading, commercials you're familiar with, movies, television shows, etc.

- Consider what the authors, illustrators, and designers are saying about *girls* and *boys*.
- How are pictures, dialogue, narrative, layout, etc., used in communicating messages?
- Think about your position in relationship to what the authors have to say.

Inside the Folder

Picture books that challenge "traditional" gender roles:

Amazing Grace by Mary Hoffman, illustrated by Caroline Binch

William's Doll by Charlotte Zolotow, illustrated by William Pene Du Bois

Benny Bakes a Cake by Eve Rice

Mama Is a Miner by George Ella Lyon, illustrated by Peter Catalanotto

Piggybook by Anthony Browne

The Paper Bag Princess by Robert Munsch

Players in Pigtails by Shana Corey, illustrated by Rebecca Gibbon

Student artifacts:

Front

BOYS	GIRLS
Peanuts 1 Boy Boys clothes looks like boy Football charlie	their girl Football looks like boy Boys clothes
Dick Tracy 7 boys front crime suit	1 girl. background shirt and skirt
2 boy messing up the House For Better or Worse	2 girls 1 girl messing up the House other cleaning For Better or Worse
Dilbert 1 boy telling in a meeting suit like a boy	Dilbert 1 girl like a girl front secratary dress

29

Other possible texts:

Comics from local Sunday newspaper (including titles like For Better or For Worse, Zits, Dilbert, Peanuts, Foxtrot)

Popular culture series books like:

Barbie Rules series; example book—*Be Your Own Best Friend* by Karen Wolcott, illustrated by Louise A. Gikow

Dora the Explorer series; example book—*Lost and Found* by Golden Books

Disney series; example book—*Disney Princess: Volume II* manufactured by Disney Press Staff

Classroom reading series basal

some way. If the party invitations have been purchased, these details might be filled in on the blank lines provided. If they have been designed by the hosts, the information might be included in a handwritten narrative or styled to match the theme of the event. In other words, there are common elements, but the actual designs can vary. The same holds true with curricular invitations—there are common, predictable structural features, but the way in which they are configured depends on the nature of the invitation and who prepares it.

Authors of a curricular invitation must decide how to include key pieces of information like the focal issue or theme, possible lines of questioning, and related resources that might be of use to those pursuing the invitation. Invitations usually have four common features:

1. An initiating experience. Initiating experiences position invitations in relation to participants' current understanding and within their social contexts. Definitions, perspectives, quotations, histories, sample scenarios, and/or questions may frame this element of the written invitation.
2. A formally presented invitation. "You are invited to" are the four words used to signify that participants are decision makers, able to chart their own course.
3. Possible questions to pursue. Since all teaching, learning, and human interactions are political, suggested questions often encourage participants to place their personal experiences within social contexts and/or approach issues from a critical perspective.
4. Related resources. Assembling diverse resources related to invitation issues facilitates rich inquiries. It is also important to allow a variety of ways in which to construct meaning—language, art, drama, mathematics, etc.

Each feature is a design element: the ways they are configured may vary from invitation to invitation, just as the key party details in a social invitation can be configured differently. The written invitation is a way of pulling together possibilities, framing thinking, and launching participants on a line of work. Thinking about these elements as guidelines reminds us that an invitation is not a set of required procedures or steps but rather an open-ended investigation that depends on the lives, experiences, and questions of those conducting it.

Once we've identified an issue of concern or interest to our students, we can begin by gathering potentially useful resources to initiate inquiry and then writing the formal invitation.

For example, the students and teachers in Room 4 were committed to creating a world that included poetry, both inside and beyond their classroom walls. Poetry was part of their daily lives. The works of Naomi Shihab Nye (2002), Billy Collins (1998), Pat Mora (2001; 1998), and other poets were read aloud, written on the message board that greeted students as they walked into the classroom each day, and used as models to inspire kids to write their own poems. Often, instead of responding to a poem in words, students would paint a visual image of what the poem brought to mind—a mood, a feeling, a swirl of colors. They were interested in the process artists went through in creating just the right hues. In light of the dominant role poetic words and images had in this classroom and the students' interest in art and social change, the teachers assembled an array of art-related resources and created the invitation Talking Back to the World Through Art.

Let's look at Talking Back to the World Through Art in terms of the architecture of an invitation:

1. *Initiating experience*. It uses quotations and examples from poets and artists to encourage students to consider multiple perspectives and purposes behind works of art.
2. *Formal invitation*. "You're invited to think about how art has been used to tell stories, capture experiences, or challenge the way things are in the world." The options listed remind participants that they have choices and that they are expected to make responsible decisions.
3. *Suggested questions for consideration*. Students are invited to read what is included in the resources, consider what is missing, make connections, and think from the artists' points of view. The final question suggests one option for action—design or (re)design.
4. *Diverse texts, tools, and resources*. The invitation includes picture books, poetry, reproductions of artworks, and past student responses. Students also have access to resources and tools not physically paired with this invitation but available within the larger context of their classroom and the school (computers, other text sets, transparencies, art supplies, media center passes, etc.).

INVITATION: Talking Back to the World Through Art

Poet Gwendolyn Brooks writes, "Art hurts. Art urges voyages."

Painter Jacob Lawrence, reflecting on his life as an artist, writes that "teachers, friends, and even actors on street corners helped me to understand how my own experiences fit into a much larger story—the history of African Americans in this country. It seemed almost inevitable that I would tell [the great migration] story in my art. . . . To me, migration means movement. While I was painting I thought about trains and people walking to the stations. I thought about field hands leaving their farms to become factory workers, and about the families that sometimes got left behind. The choices made were hard ones, so I wanted to show what made the people get on those northbound trains. I also wanted to show just what it cost to ride them. . . ."

Poet Ntozake Shange invites artist Romare Bearden to respond in image to the poem that she has composed to celebrate the language of music. Her use of image-filled language like, "sound/ falls round me like rain" helps Bearden "sing on canvas." Both this poet and this artist give life to issues and eras that some may think of as frozen pieces of the past meant for textbooks, monuments, or street signs.

You're invited to think about how art has been used to tell stories, capture experiences, or challenge the way things are in the world.

As you explore works of art, you might think about:

- What do these works of art make you think of?
- What do you think is or isn't being said through these works of art?
- What might the artists have hoped to say about their lives or world?
- What do you think these pieces of art say about the world?
- How might you use art to talk back to important issues?

Resources

Picture Books

Story Painter: The Life of Jacob Lawrence by John Duggleby and Jacob Lawrence

Romare Bearden: Collage of Memories by Jan Greenberg, illustrated by Romare Bearden

The Great Migration: An American Story by Jacob Lawrence with opening poem by Walter Dean Myers

Frida by Jonah Winter, illustrated by Ana Juan

Poetry Picture Book
Black Cat by Christopher Myers

I Live in Music by Ntozake Shange, edited by Linda Sunshine, illustrated by
   Romare Bearden

Ellington Was Not a Street by Ntozake Shange, illustrated by Kadir Nelson

Artifacts

Postcard, Internet printouts, calendars such as *Women and Art* calendar and
   Art from the United States, available from the Art Institute of Chicago,
   www.artic.edu/aic/students/resources.html

Jacob Lawrence: Book of Postcards, www.karibugifts.com/
   jacoblawrence1.html

Diego Rivera Postcards, Diego Rivera Web Museum, www.diegorivera.com

Mexican Mural Paintings by Rivera, Orozco and Siqueiros by Dover Publi-
   cations, available through Amazon.com

Art Sites

The Whitney Museum of American Art, New York City, www.whitney.org

The Smithsonian Museum, Washington, D.C., www.si.edu

Artcyclopedia, www.artcyclopedia.com

The Worldwide Art Gallery, www.theartgallery.com.au/

Depending on the experience and ability of the readers in our classroom, we might create written invitations using words and icons, or we might audiotape initial invitations. As for resources, we might pay extra attention to their diversity, so that they include a variety of printed texts as well as audio recordings, visual diagrams, and art works. An example of an invitation whose text and resources could engage more emergent readers appears on the next page.

Giving Students Choices About Which Invitation to Pursue

In order to choose an invitation, students need to know which ones are available. They can learn this in various ways. Depending on the experience of our readers, we might first read each formal invitation aloud. Students might also learn about available invitations by way of invitation talks, through related experiences, or by returning to the invitation over several work periods.

Invitation Talks

New invitations can be introduced by their creator (teacher or student). These short book-talk-like introductions can be windows into potential lines of inquiry. Chapter 1 mentioned Emily's interest in the transcontinental railroad and her intention to create an invitation related to a book she'd read and in a format with which she was familiar. After creating a multiple-viewpoints invitation (see pages 35 to 38) related to the transcontinental railroad, Emily introduced the invitation to her classmates with the following talk:

> In May of 1869 they finished building the first railroad that went across the United States. Our social studies book tells about the ceremony at Promontory Point when they finally finished building the tracks, but there's more you should know—like strikes, attacks, and worries about the railroad and slavery. You're invited to explore the Chinese perspective, the viewpoints of the Irish workers and the railroad company owners, and more. Was it just about building a railroad to connect the coasts of what is now the United States of America?

Linked Experiences

Because new invitations are often linked to events in students' lives, another way students can come to know about an invitation's focus is through daily interactions with a familiar issue. For example, in Room 4 the In the News invitation was based on recent newspaper feature articles. The articles included had been mentioned during the morning meeting and were being talked about throughout the day. Many of the students had read some of the articles, either at home or at school, and had questions about them. All these experiences helped students get a sense of what the invitation was about and the kind of things they might explore if they signed up for it.

INVITATION: If the World Were a Village

You're invited to explore languages spoken in the world. Before you begin, you might:

- Predict the languages spoken most in the world.
- Predict the languages spoken in your city/state.
- Talk about why you made your predictions.

Look at the marked pages in *If the World Were a Village* and *If Illinois Were a Village* table with information about Illinois.

If Illinois Were a Village Languages Spoken Would Be . . .

Languages	Total No. of speakers in Illinois	If 100 people lived in Illinois
English only	9,326,786	81
Spanish	1,253,676	11
European Languages: French, French Creole, Italian, Portuguese, German, Yiddish, Russian, Serbo-Croation, Persian, Gujarathi, Polish, Armenian, Hindi, Urdu . . .	640,237	6
Asian and Pacific Languages: Chinese, Japanese, Korean, Cambodian, Hmong, Thai, Laotian, Vietnamese, Tagalog, other Pacific languages . . .	248,800	2
Other languages: Navajo, Native North American languages, Hungarian, Arabic, Hebrew, African languages . . .	74,664	$\frac{1}{2}$

2000 Census results for languages spoken in Illinois
2000 total population: 12,419,293.
2000 total population five years and over: 11,547,505

To understand the numbers, you might want to use Unifix cubes to represent Illinois and the world. What do you notice? What questions come to mind? What can you learn?

Based on what you found out today, what might you do?

Resource
If the World Were a Village: A Book About the World's People, by David Smith, illustrated by Shelagh Armstrong

INVITATION: Transcontinental Railroad

What is now known as the Transcontinental Railroad was built between 1863 and 1869. Its construction affected the lives of many people, including those who actually worked to build it, those who lived on the land where the tracks were being laid, those who financed and profited from it, and those who made decisions about the building the United States of America.

You're invited to learn more about the Transcontinental Railroad, including:

- the events that came before its construction,
- the important issues and challenges that came up as plans were made and tracks laid, and
- the decisions made by workers, railroad company bosses, Native Americans, and members of the U.S. government.

Before you begin exploring the resources included with this invitation, select one of the following roles. Then explore the building of the Transcontinental Railroad from the perspective of your role. Remember, the viewpoints held by the role you choose might not be the same as your opinion or perspective. Invite group members to take on different roles so that you can explore this issue from multiple perspectives.

Resources

Picture Books
Railroad Fever: Building the Transcontinental Railroad 1830–1870 by Monica Halpern

Ten Mile Day: The Building of the Transcontinental Railroad by Mary Ann Fraiser

Polly Bemis: A Chinese American Pioneer by Priscilla Wegars

Coolies by Lee Patricia Yin, illustrated by Chris K. Soentpiet

Text Books
A More Perfect Union, Houghton Mifflin, pp. 418–419

America Will Be, Houghton Mifflin, pp. 480–481

Websites
Central Pacific Railroad, http://cprr.org/

PBS, "Transcontinental Railroad: American Experience," www.pbs.org/wgbh/amex/tcrr/

Video
Chi, M., M. Zwonitzer, directors, and M. Murphy, narrator. *The Transcontinental Railroad.* PBS Home Video, 2003.

Roles

Worker for the Central Pacific Railroad: Many of the Central Pacific employees were immigrants. They worked to build the railroad starting in the West and moving East. In the beginning there many were Irish workers. Over time, the company needed more workers. They began to hire Chinese immigrants at low wages. The company also knew that if they started to hire Chinese workers, the Irish would worry that they might lose their jobs altogether and would stop asking for better money and working conditions.

Worker for the Union Pacific Railroad: These workers started in what is now the mid-section of the United States. When the Civil War ended, the Union Pacific recruited many war veterans to work for the railroad along with Irish immigrants. When Jack Casement was the construction boss, building the railroad was run a lot like the military. Men had specific jobs (like spikeman, hammer-wielders, etc.) and came to know their boss as "General Jack."

Native American: In 1846 the United States added Texas to its territory after the war with Mexico. California became a new state in 1850. As the U.S. continued to expand, land was being taken from others, including many different Native American tribes. Conflicts, major and minor, arose during the construction of the railroad.

Railroad Businessmen: Shortly after California became a state, a man who came to be known as Crazy Judah wanted to build a railroad from Embarcadero, CA to the foothills to accommodate the Gold Rush. He and many other businessmen to follow traveled back and forth between New York, Washington, and the railroad sites trying to convince the government to go ahead with the railroad and to find money to help pay for the project. Many of these men made large amounts of money from the construction of the Transcontinental Railroad.

President of the United States: The railroad took years to build and involved decisions made by congressmen, senators, and the presidents. During the major years of construction the presidents included James Buchanan, Abraham Lincoln, and Andrew Johnson. Many of the railroad businessmen went to the government for money, land, and support for building the railroad.

Wife of an Irish Union Pacific Railroad worker: Many of the Irish workers who flocked to the central United States to help build the railroad had to leave their wives and children behind in east-coast cities like New York and

Boston for months at a time. This often meant the wives were left to do the work of both parents, take care of the money, protect the children, and make sure there was enough food at a time when it was unusual for a woman to be the head of a household.

As you explore resources, you could make notes from the perspective of the role you picked using colored post-its.

Working with Known Invitations

Yet another way students can become aware of an invitation is by having participated in it earlier and choosing to revisit it. Returning to an invitation for several consecutive sessions encourages students to work with classmates over time. Longer periods of collaborative work often add greater depth to students' inquiries. Students make plans, gather materials, and work through the challenges of following through on a charted agenda.

Students may also elect to participate in the same invitation with different group members. For example, Maria was a frequent Mother's Day–Ads participant. For two weeks she worked with Shelly to create a bilingual Power-Point presentation detailing the similarities and differences between Mexican and American notions of Mother's Day/día de las madres. Another week she worked with Jackie, suggesting possible issues they might pursue together. Repeating an invitation can lead to new learning, invite thinking from different perspectives, and offer students different learner roles depending on the experiences of the students with whom they're working each time.

Learning from Presentations

Lastly, students may develop familiarity with invitations because of their friends' and classmates' experiences in working on them. Invitations are typically followed by reflection and debriefing (detailed in later sections of this chapter). As students listen and respond to their peers' work (analyzing political cartoons, critiquing book orders, researching and writing a survival book, etc.) during these minipresentations, they make mental or physical notes (see Figure 3–1) that may influence which invitations they choose in the future.

Establishing Sign-Up Procedures

After we've put together enough invitations so that all of our students can gather in small work groups, they need to select the invitation that appeals to them. We want students to choose which invitation to take up, and we want them to follow through on the choices they've made. Developing sign-up procedures encourages students to make and stick with their commitments.

Sign-up procedures should suit the class' needs. Systems can range from a simple list of available invitations on a whiteboard where students can write their name next to the one they wish to pursue to a chart in which students can tuck a card with their name on it into the pocket bearing the name of the invitation they want to work on (see Figure 3–2).

To facilitate productive group work, we can include with each invitation title a small number indicating the ideal number of students who should work on it. These numbers are only guidelines and are most useful when determined by the class. If there are more students interested than the assigned number, two or more groups can work on the same invitation, or perhaps the class will decide that a larger group is feasible and productive.

FIGURE 3–1. Nina's notes from invitation presentations

FIGURE 3–2. Sample invitations sign-up board

Making Invitations Interesting and Engaging

Students and teachers need to share a vision of literacy that includes using it to create a better world. Both teachers and students need to know that invitations are not about seeking right answers or rushing to be done; rather, invitations are experiences in which learners, working together, reach new insights that lead them to take action. Therefore, the invitations offered need to connect with the surrounding social worlds in ways that maintain the genuine complexities of the issues at hand.

Consider how the students in the following vignette connect their questions with real-world complexities as they explore "answers" and ask new questions that move beyond the immediate context of the invitation. This group of fourth, fifth, and sixth graders is interested in learning about language. Their work on previous invitations has generated questions about Ebonics. After conducting a Google search, they print an article from the Center for Applied Linguistics and slowly and deliberately begin to read the opening paragraphs aloud. Stopping frequently to talk through what they are reading, they share what they think the article is about and ask many questions as they try to navigate the academic discourse in which the article is written. This article isn't intended for fourth-, fifth-, and sixth-grade readers, yet their persistent questions keep them interested and engaged. While they gain some new insights about Ebonics, their definitions and understanding are still fuzzy. But as they continue, an important question surfaces: "Why is it written like this?" Missy asks. A classmate responds, "Maybe it's only meant for certain people to read." Their inquiry shifts. They now want to know why people write articles, books, and advertisements in such a way that only certain groups of people can understand them. Deeper into this conversation, questions like "Who decides what's proper?" and "Why don't people think kids are interested?" are asked and debated.

These students start off with a focusing question generated by earlier invitation work. They want to understand what Ebonics is and isn't. Their research leads to helpful information as well as new questions. The difficulty and authenticity of their inquiry sustains their involvement. While their new understanding doesn't mirror the sophistication of linguists, they certainly have a better idea not only of Ebonics but of how and why language is used in particular ways and what that means to a reader. Interest and engagement are connected to agency and choice. The students begin with *their* questions, which have been inspired by earlier questions raised by their teacher and peers. The invitation broadly frames their work, but they are in charge of paving their inquiry paths.

In invitations, students craft flexible and purposeful agendas; they know that the focus of their work may vary as they move forward, make new discoveries, and interact with different groups of students. Interest and engagement hinge on group decision making and a genuinely complex pursuit of issues pertinent to their lives.

While it's safe to say that no two invitation groups engage in the same activity, there are some common practices that help groups come to shared agendas and collective action. Generally speaking, when an invitation group gathers, their initial time together is spent exploring and thinking about the directions they might head. This entails reading the formal invitation and sifting through the resources provided. Then, with an evolving agenda in mind, work begins. Together, students talk, make use of the available resources (the library, the computer center, the art center, nearby classmates) to make continual progress.

Building in Opportunities for Reflection

Part of creating visions of what is possible involves taking the time to step back, consider the process, ponder important discoveries or accomplishments, and plan future work. Reflection can take many forms, but establishing a predictable structure or routine helps students use the time productively. Using a form, learning log, or similar strategy enables students to look back without worrying about procedures. These aids are not intended to be worksheets or writing prompts; rather, they provide the space and the opportunity to write and sketch one's thoughts and reactions, thus increasing participants' awareness of their decisions, insights, and learning journeys. Students can then draw on these tools as they share the processes and products of their work with others.

Reflection Forms

Reflection forms invite students to look back on the work they did, both the process and what they discovered, from a number of perspectives. For example:

- List two things you learned today that you didn't know before.
- Map your group work—what did you do today?
- Reflect on your role(s) in the work you did today.
- Record new questions that you have as a result of your work.
- Make a sketch that represents your work today.
- What key points about your work today should others know about?
- Create plans for your next work session.

These prompts are intended to initiate thinking and should be modified to best fit a particular group of learners. Reflection is meant to be brief—we're not asking students to justify or put down on paper everything they did. We want them to look back, identify important moments, and consider what their actions mean in terms of future actions. A sample reflection form and examples of reflection forms are shown in Figure 3–3. Look at how Steve uses a reflection form to replay parts of his work and how Nina includes beliefs and understanding grown from her group work. Amy uses a picture illustrating overlapping voices to capture the energetic tone of her group's

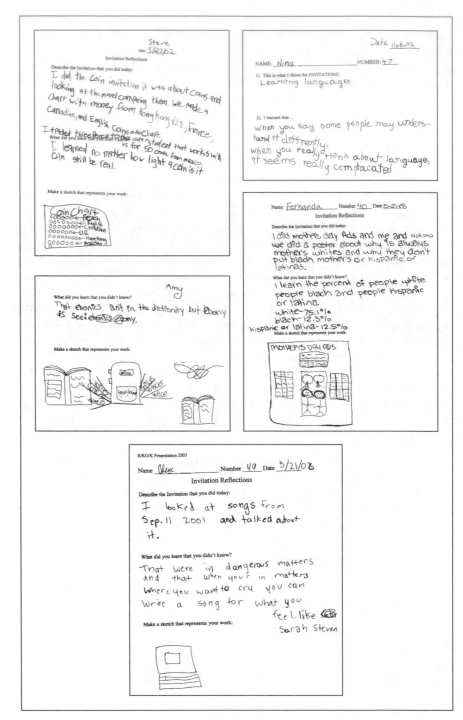

FIGURE 3–3. Invitation student samples and reflections form

Name _____ Date _____

Invitation Reflections

The invitation I chose to work with today was

_____.

I learned that:

_____

_____

_____

_____

_____

Now, I wonder:

_____

_____

_____

_____

Create a picture and/or image to represent your experiences.

You may use the back to take notes during presentations.

FIGURE 3–3. *Continued*

work. Fernanda records findings, and Alex makes connections between her work and future actions.

Learning Logs

As invitations become an integral part of the curriculum, we may want students to set aside a folder or notebook dedicated specifically to them—a place in which they take notes as they work on invitations and gather their thinking about what they discover. They could also use their learning logs as a site for narrative reflections. We may want to generate a menu of potential reflection prompts like those listed on page 41 in the discussion of reflection forms. We might also remind students to review their notes as they reflect and invite them to mark points they want to remember or explore further (see Figure 3–4).

Partnered Responses

All reflection need not be individual. We should invite students to take five minutes or so to have a written conversation with a classmate—one in their group or in a different group—about the work. Figure 3–5 shows some ways that primary and intermediate students thought through their work as they talked with a classmate. Colin and Mindy had been working together on the same invitation; Stephen and Bridgette had been working on different invitations.

All reflection need not be done on paper either. We might ask students to apply the "think-pair-share" technique: students pair up; think/write/ sketch about their invitation work; talk with their partner for a few minutes about their work, processes, and discoveries; and then share with the whole class in a group discussion. Having everyone first say something about their

FIGURE 3–4. Primary and intermediate narrative invitation reflections

 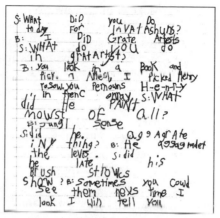

FIGURE 3-5. Students' written conversation reflections

work to a partner can greatly improve whole-group discussions, in terms of how many students participate and the quality of what they say.

Whether we choose to create reflection forms, use ongoing learning logs, or invite students to think with others about their work, we need to be cautious about two things. First, reflections are brief and do not represent everything that has transpired during a particular invitation. Second, reflections cannot be the only means we use to evaluate the legitimacy of student work. They are a tool to help learners sort through the day's events, select moments of significance, and designate focal points that they want to follow up on or share with their classmates.

Sharing Thinking, Experiences, Insights, and Processes

Learners can share their insights with classmates through minipresentations that convey important insights and/or capture important processes. As the name implies, minipresentations are short and informal. Students might share artifacts they have created (transparencies, computer slides, posters), talk from their notes, pose questions to the whole class for feedback, or describe their journey. Presentations focus on content when students bring issues to the class for feedback and perspective. They focus on student processes when they lay out the decisions that have been made and the additional inquiries that will be made.

Effective minipresentations might:

- Summarize activity: "Today we . . . "
- Raise awareness: "Do you know that everyone in the world doesn't have access to clean water?"
- Share surprises: "Did you know that Dr. Seuss was a political cartoonist?"

- Make connections: "What we were talking about today, Standard English and Ebonics, is related to the movie *Roots*."
- Pose questions: "What do you think this political cartoon means?"
- Survey classmates: "How many of you are wearing shirts that were made in Asia or Latin America?"
- Look ahead: "Next time we're planning to . . . "
- Communicate findings and processes: "We had to go to the dictionary because none of us understood how some people can row with a single scull and the pictures weren't enough."
- Solicit broader involvement: "We're forming a committee; who would like to join?"
- Perform excerpts of the activity: "Today we put music and poems together, here's an example."
- Ask new questions: "Now we want to know, 'What are musical rhythms like in other cultures?'"

This sharing is more than reporting or telling, it's taking action and sparking conversations about important issues or learning processes. Therefore, we also need to think about how audience and presenters interact. Listeners can raise questions about students' thinking and suggest new resources. While compliments are always welcome, we need to move the conversation beyond "You worked hard today" to be more specific about the moves we value: "Your sources produced information and stories that didn't match up. Figuring out possible reasons is important. Has anyone else experienced this? Is anyone else working on an invitation that might benefit from looking at multiple sources at the same time?"

Invitations never stand alone. Minipresentations are one way for students to see options for new invitations as well as connections between invitations. They are opportunities to highlight student moves and decisions that other students can try in upcoming work. Lasty, the act of talking about collaborative work gives us another opportunity to assess progress and note challenges that we may want to focus on during future work.

INVITATIONS FOR ALL

Thinking Through the Conditions and Decisions That Support Invitations in Your Classroom

The following list of questions will help you think through your next steps. Read through them, and jot down notes, responses, and ideas you want to remember.

How can you regularly incorporate invitations into your teaching?

Where will invitation groups work? How will work areas be determined and communicated?

What larger classroom procedures need to be considered to support invitations?

How can students access additional resources?

In what ways can students use technology to aid them in their inquiries?

How are materials such as art supplies dealt with in your classroom?

How will invitation work be organized? Where will the products generated be kept?

How will you apply the architectural framework as you create invitations in your classroom? Who will design and author invitations with you?

How and when will you introduce invitations? What sign-up procedures will you establish?

How will your students reflect on their work?

In what ways can students share their work?

How and where will you fit in? How will you communicate and play your roles (kidwatcher, co-participant, etc.)?

4 Identifying Issues, Themes, and Possibilities

Articulating our hopes and dreams for students as critically literate people helps us begin to see different curricular options as we inquire into students' lives, learn about the resources students bring into our classrooms, and discover the issues on our students' minds. We begin to see things like playground bullying not as isolated incidents in need of immediate adult resolution ("Apologize" or "Don't say that again") but as curricular opportunities. When children raise difficult questions like "If we have the United Nations, why can't we have a united world?" we don't see these wonderings as "too big" for answers but as complex curricular options in a world filled with difficult issues and complex problems that don't have easy, singular, or immediate answers. Since we cannot know for certain what problems our students will encounter or what content will be useful in the course of their constantly unfolding lives, we need to be learners alongside our students. We need to look at ourselves as well as at them.

We can begin by reflecting on the ways in which we are or might become critical readers and actors in our own lives. As we engage in ongoing professional conversations and rethink the relationships between our beliefs and practices, we must articulate visions for being and becoming literate. What is literacy about and for? What will students think it is about and for as a result of their experiences in our classrooms? How can we find out what issues matter to the students in our classrooms? And what decisions can we make to offer the best learning opportunities for our students?

Combining our vision for literate citizens, our own literacy practices, and the things we learn about our students, we can construct critical curricular invitations that prompt students to become active learners, critical consumers, sustained contemplators, and agents of change. With these goals in mind, it seems logical to focus on questions like:

- How do we identify the issues that matter to the students in our classrooms?
- How do we invite students to make use of their lived experiences and cultural resources in the course of their inquiries?

- How do we encourage students to wonder, inquire, explore, and question issues that matter to them?
- How do we support students' sustained inquiries and interests in social action as we learn from the directions they take while responding to an invitation?

Invitations offer a space for further dialogue and thinking about the things that weigh on students' minds. To create engaging invitations, we need to observe and reflect on our students' lives. We need to construct invitations related to what we learn about and from our students, and then observe with watchful, informed eyes as students work with those invitations.

Beginning with the Known

We have to begin somewhere, and curriculum should begin with students' current experiences. Short, Harste, and Burke (1988, 1996) talk about "building from the known." They emphasize the importance of starting with curricular engagements that have multiple points of entry that enable students, from the least to most proficient, to participate in meaningful literate activity. All children carry experiences with them when they enter our classrooms, and one of our tasks is to discover what those experiences are. We then must apply this thinking to critical invitations, beginning with local issues, interests, and experiences so that all students have something to share. Background knowledge, then, isn't something we provide for students, it's something we build on.

Learning about our students' lives also means angling our inquiries toward issues or themes rather than events, topics, or ideas. While this might at first seem like a minor difference in wording, events, topics, and ideas are often singular or constraining. For example, it would be more productive and engaging to take up the issue of bullying on the playground than to single out the one time a group of older girls picked on the first graders. Locating the incident within a larger social context brings up issues about age and power that may help students live differently not only on the playground but in the world. Themes or issues encourage thinking about big ideas filled with real tensions that spur real questions. Tensions and questions, versus inquiries with predetermined factual answers, complicate inquiries and invite sustained engagement.

If we're to build from the known, we have to start with options that invite all learners. When I think about building a cohesive learning community, I think about curricular engagements that are aimed at getting to know members of the community. While finding out who read Harry Potter over the summer, who loves pizza, or who owns a dog may be good things to know, I prefer engagements that take students beyond lists and into activity that provides insights into their lives and their thinking.

For example, names are one of the first things that come to mind when building a new community. One might wonder, "What are the names of the members of our class?" This question falls under the heading or topic of names but doesn't lead to deep learning about community members. We can think of names as rote words that we commit to memory, or we can think of them as more complex entities that represent stories, tensions, and experiences—who we are. Instead of a finite answer-oriented question, we might ask, "What stories do our names hold?" "Why are some people teased about their name?" "What do our names tell or not tell others about who we are?" "Are some last names derived from occupations?" These kinds of questions welcome thinking about names from many different perspectives—as not just a personal possession but also a symbol of who we are and can be in various social settings. Exploring the stories surrounding our names invites contemplating and questioning the social practices (like name calling and name changes) that reveal how our cultural life and identity are tied up with the word we refer to as our name.

Framing an invitation around student names can open up a broad range of experiences that can be a catalyst for other invitations connected to the stories told and questions asked. The What's in a Name? invitation includes suggestions for picture book and poetry resources. Depending on the students we're working with, we could also include tape recordings of someone reading the books and poems, name cards with digital photos of each class member, or more name-related poetry.

Remember, this invitation is just one possible point of departure to prompt thinking about issues that reach across all class members and their lived experiences. If offered at the beginning of the school year, the invitation might help the classroom community become more cohesive. Another option is to pick up on the interests already present in our students' lives and direct students toward activity that will reveal more about the issues and thinking weighing on their minds.

Gathering Data and Making Decisions

The students in Room 4 had an avid interest in maps. Students used the giant world map on the wall to search for several classmates' native pueblos in Mexico; locate one child's family home in Algeria; retrace the routes of slave ships; discover the relationships between longitude and time; investigate the connections between currency from Belize, Hong Kong, Canada, and Britain; and question colonialism in the world today.

This collective interest in maps led Shelia to the public library with her grandmother to investigate Algeria, Israel, and Mexico (countries from which three of her classmates had emigrated). She brought the resources to school and with her classmates pored over the books and maps and discussed climactic differences. Another student, Sara, took time early in the year to record her observations of the map on the wall—writing what she saw and thought in Arabic. Her writer's notebook entry (Figure 4–1) demonstrates

Sara's emergent understanding of classroom practices that value making meaning across languages and sign systems.

As these students worked with maps, their teacher listened to their conversations, perused their writing, and made notes about their questions and interests. Based on her observations, she decided to create an invitation focused on maps (see page 53). While it is certainly anchored in the known for many students, it offers many opportunities for future learning. The invitation leads kids in possible directions rather than mandates previously paved paths, and it informs future curricular decisions.

Over time, Shelly, Gino, Jessica, Brian, Ana Cristina, and Anthony all worked with the My Maps invitation. While each of their experiences included mapmaking, what they revealed about themselves as learners and

FIGURE 4–1. Sara's map writing

people varied. Shelly first drew a map of herself, labeling details like her freckles, then created a map of her bedroom. When she shared her bedroom map (Figure 4–2), she pointed out a new hot-pink bed that was not hers but that of the daughter of her mother's boyfriend. Gino's map of his family (Figure 4–3) included siblings and cousins that lived with him, and after he had said all their names he talked about family members that remained miles away in Mexico. Jessica's map of her day (Figure 4–4) revealed the rigor of her academic and musical studies at home, which included learning English and practicing to become an accomplished violinist. Ana Cristina's map blended together elements of her Mexican neighborhood and new friends in her current classroom. The two-level "blueprint" Anthony created initiated conversations about his current living arrangements, his mother's continued search for a better job, and the ongoing tension created by a possible move to a new house or apartment. Brian pulled together his technological talents, his ongoing interest in playground games, and his cartography skills to map key locations for recess games (Figure 4–5).

Clearly, the tangible artifacts produced by invitations are wonderful tools for learning more about our students. Adding what these maps tell us about students to ongoing lists of what we already know about them (see Figure 4–6) reveals additional curricular options connected to the tensions and issues our students face. Shelly was about to experience a change in the makeup of her family; Gino's life was challenged by distance and borders; Jessica was balancing academic and parental demands in a new culture; Ana

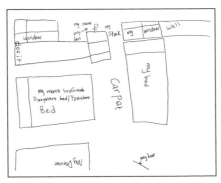

FIGURE 4–2. Shelly's map of her bedroom

FIGURE 4–3. Gino's map

Cartographers are people who make maps. They create maps to provide information about the earth in easily understandable forms. Working closely with others (surveyors, geologists, etc.) their aim is to develop accurate and useful road maps, climactic maps, bus route maps, and so on. Maps might be created for pilots, ship's captains, tourists, and/or mountain climbers. They might portray information like routes, altitude, specific locations, etc., in visual form. The type of map created depends on intended audience, information to be shared, and the available tools for mapmaking.

You're invited to browse the map resources at this invitation. Notice the different kinds of information communicated through the maps. Ponder the following questions as you decide upon a direction for your work:

Does one kind of map appeal to you?

What do these maps tell you? What do they not tell you?

Are there other different kinds of maps that might be included?

How could you design a similar map? How could you create a different map?

As you read, discuss, and/or create, think about the connections between purpose, design, and possible readings.

Resources

Picture Books
My Map Book by Susan Fanelli
National Geographic Beginner's World Atlas by National Geographic Society
Small Worlds: Maps and Map Making by Karen Romano Young

Artifacts
Other various maps which might include physical maps, pictorial maps of amusement parks or museums from brochures, maps of subway or train lines, airport layout maps, etc.

Cristina was looking for ways to bring together her Mexico neighborhood and her school community; Anthony was worrying about salaries, bills, and a possible move; and Brian was eager to engage others in more organized recess play. This kind of information might not have been immediately apparent in classroom conversations or student writing: Gino and Anthony rarely shared their thinking verbally; Jessica was an emergent writer of conventional

FIGURE 4–4. Jessica's map of her day

FIGURE 4–5. Brian's map of the playground with game locations

English; Shelly struggled with articulating her thoughts clearly in writing. The many points of entry and departure in the maps invitation suggest future critical invitations in which these students can learn more about language and literacy practices as they use a broader range of practices to encode, decode, critique, and act on the issues that permeate their lives.

Student	Grade	Language(s) Spoken	What I know about their cultural lives, experiences and resources that they bring to the classroom
Shelly	5	English	• Loves music—records song lyrics in writer's notebook, covers binders with musical group logos (writer's notebook) • Is a literary borrower—uses other texts as models to support her writing, not one to write extended narratives on her own (writer's notebook) • Has moved between several local schools (school records)

FIGURE 4–6. Student data chart

Student	Grade	Language(s) Spoken	*What I know about their cultural lives, experiences and resources that they bring to the classroom*
Shelly	5	English	• During a conference her mom shares that she now sees Shelly as a writer, noting her own love for storytelling and writing (family/teacher interaction) • Shelly's older brother attends many school functions with her mother (family/teacher interaction) • Working with classmates, Shelly is trying to learn Spanish (observational notes) • *Shelly's family structure is changing (My Maps invitation)*
Gino	4	Spanish	• Loves to draw—he has a folder of Digimon and Pokemon drawings that he carries to and from school each day, he signs notes using a cartoon logo, classmates turn to him to learn how to draw cartoon images (observational notes) • Writes about lived experiences comparing Mexico and Newtown—his experiences are written in his first language, Spanish, then English (writer's notebook and drafts) • He is expecting a new sibling to be born soon (family/teacher interaction) • *His local household consists of extended family and now I have a clear image of those in Mexico and those that interact with him daily (My Maps invitation)*
Jessica	6	Korean	• Lives with her aunt and cousin who is also studying violin (family/teacher interactions) • Teaches classmates to draw anime like characters (observational notes, writer's notebooks) • Uses her Korean mainly to teach others how to write particular characters (classmates' writer's notebooks) • Writes with many approximations toward conventional English (writer's notebook)

FIGURE 4–6. *Continues*

Student	Grade	Language(s) Spoken	What I know about their cultural lives, experiences and resources that they bring to the classroom
Jessica	6	Korean	• *Surprises her classmates with the rigor of her study and days (My Maps invitation)*
Brian	4	English	• Chooses to engage in activity related to building things—legos, etc. (choice time, indoor recess)
			• Relates to pop culture worlds including video games, Digimon, and Lord of the Rings (writer's notebook, class meetings)
			• Participates in inventing and playing in recess games (playground observations)
			• *Understands communicative purposes and potentials of maps as he uses his map to support evolving rules and moves associated with playground games (My Maps invitation)*

FIGURE 4–6. *Continued*

Moving Beyond the Known

Invitations are also opportunities for students to delve deeper into issues in their lives or engage in comparative discussions about their experiences and relationships. To help them dig deeper, we need to look within and beyond the invitation activities we offer. Using students' interests and resources as a starting point, we must pay attention to the social issues that surround us and them. We need to introduce other ways of seeing, suggest anomalies, and prompt student thinking that moves beyond what they currently know to situate their thinking socially as they ponder new possibilities regarding how the world *is* and *could be*.

Finding out what's on our students' minds requires attending to student-produced artifacts, student talk, and student actions. For example, students may make their thinking visible on paper, writing about issues of inequity (see Figure 4–7), differences of opinion (see Figure 4–8), political positions (see Figure 4–9), and environmental concerns (see Figure 4–10).

However, many issues and questions are raised in ways other than writing. Students chat together on the way in from the bus, make comments to friends seated near them during self-selected reading (SSR), interact on the playground, have conversations during morning meeting, speak with one another in the lunch line, and talk with tablemates as they write or work on projects. When we listen carefully to students' words and attend closely to their actions, we discover that while sometimes students' ques-

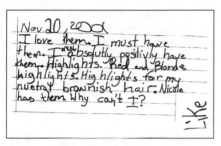

> Nov 20, 200d
> I love them. I must have
> them. I must absolutly positivly have
> them. Highlights. Red and Blonde
> highlights. Highlights for my
> nuetral brownish hair. Nicole
> has them. Why can't I?
> Like

FIGURE 4–7. Alissa's hair writing

> MY Opinion
> Me and my parents have a very
> different opinion on one thing.
> VIDEO GAMES
> I really like them but my really
> hate them (well they don't really
> hate them they just don't like
> them)....

FIGURE 4–8. Mark's video games
writing

> war or peace
> I think that religions
> does not matter.
> This only makes more
> wars.
> I hate wars I love
> peace.
> But there were people that
> want more land.
> They are trying take it by fighting but
> the people who fight vuught gets killed.

FIGURE 4–8. Nina's war and peace
writing

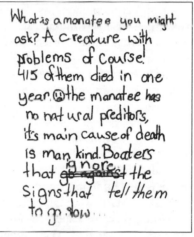

> What is a manatee you might
> ask? A creature with
> problems of course!
> 415 of them died in one
> year. 2 the manatee has
> no natural preditors,
> it's main cause of death
> is man kind. Boaters
> that ignore the
> signs that tell them
> to go slow...

FIGURE 4–10. Mindy's manatee
writing

tions are explicit and easily recognized (see Mark's writing about video games in Figure 4–8 and Mindy's research-informed concern for environmentally threatened manatees in Figure 4–10), issues are also tucked inside larger conversations or interactions.

For example, one day Room 4 members were discussing a biracial student's decision to straighten her hair in order to look more like her white friends. This conversation led to further questioning about hair and beauty. Like Alissa's notebook entry (see Figure 4–7), their initial talk was anchored in the personal as they shared related stories and opinions. However, as they continued talking, their thinking moved beyond personal fairness to center on how beauty is defined and who defines it. Their noticing, questions, and comments contained the potential for additional inquiries about race, identity, and dominant images of beauty.

What is important here is not only how we identify the issues weighing on our students' minds but what we do with them once we have. Do we let them pass? Do we respond with comments like, "Her hair was beautiful before, too; we're all beautiful in our own way" or "You're not old enough for highlights"? Or do we push students further and help them explore new ways of interpreting and acting within a given context or scenario?

Connecting Data to New Invitations

Invitations are opportunities for students to extend and question their thinking. They're a time to engage in extended inquiry and explore one's initial beliefs and understanding. Invitations are places where students like Nina (see Figure 4–9) can begin with personal positions on war, religion, and peace, read related poetry, gather information about past and current conflicts, and contemplate how they (like other writers, activists, politicians, artists) might use writing (art, speech) as peace-urging tools.

There are many places we can learn about our students' lives and then use what we learn to make relevant curricular decisions. Applying this stance to the hair-related issues buzzing around Room 4 in student writing, hallway talk, and morning meeting discussions, the teachers created the invitation on the next page.

Creating Invitations in Response to Casual Conversations and Passing Comments

Casual comments or interactions are often the best means of discovering what is on students' minds. At the end of one afternoon, Colin, Mindy, Nina, and Maria were talking as Maria sat cutting a "snowflake" design from a colored piece of paper. Mindy commented, "Oh it's a colored snowflake, only it's a rectangle." Maria replied that it wasn't a snowflake. As she held it up, her tablemates guessed it was a flag. When Maria explained that it was *papel picado* for a celebration, her classmates wanted to know more about this traditional Mexican art. Days later, Magic Windows became an invitation option (see page 61), as students were invited to move beyond their first impression of a colored, rectangular snowflake to a new understanding of their classmate's culture. Working with this invitation encouraged students to examine the cultural lenses through which they see and read what surrounds them. They began to resee, reread, and retrace the things that inform how they perceive and make judgments about the world.

Creating Invitations in Response to Student Writing

Andréa was a reflective thinker, writer, and inquirer. Through the pages of her writing notebook, her teachers discovered her attention to the world around her as well as her hopes for social change. It was filled with entries about her early life in Brazil, her health, her adoption, learning English, life's changes and challenges, and the power of writing. The entry in Figure 4–11 led to the invitation on page 63.

One of my greatest joys is writing picture books. I have discovered the pleasures of telling a story of happiness or sorrow in a few simple words. I like to write picture books that make young people ponder, that encourage them to ask questions. "Why did that happen, Mom? Could it happen again? Can't we help? What can we do?" (Eve Bunting www.kidsreads.com/authors/au-bunting-eve.asp)

Eve Bunting writes as a way to encourage people to ask questions. So do the authors of the books listed below.

You're invited to read these books, examine the illustrations, and look at the work of your peers that is included in this folder. What do these things make you think about? What questions come to mind?

You might consider questions like these:

- Why is it like that?
- What can we do?
- What do we think?
- Why did that happen?

- Why do people think this way?
- Could it happen again?
- Can we help?
- Is it important to our lives now?

Sketch or write about your thoughts/questions.

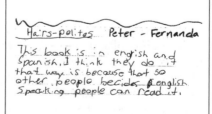

```
thought  Philippines have tuned skin
quiton  why does she care about what
        other people think about her
quiton  why did he call her wild child.
quiton  why did she stay under the covers.
thought monday was the day she got her
        hair braded.
quiton  why would she hide from her
        father.
thought She was dis plesed of her hair.
quiton  why does she not whant her mother
        to brad her hair.
answer  she thinks it will hurt.
thought her hair was all happy his
amazes  first they comeb the hair then
```

```
Hairs-polites   Peter - Fernanda

This book is in english and
spanish, I think they do it
that way is because that so
other people becids english
speaking people can read it.
```

Artifacts

Resources

I Love My Hair! by Natasha Anastasia Tarpley, illustrated by E. B. Lewis

Erandi's Braids by Antonio Hernández Madrigal, illustrated by Tomie de Paola

Hairs/Pelitos by Sandra Cisneros

Wild, Wild Hair by Nikki Grimes, illustrated by George Ford

Nappy Hair by Carolivia Herron, illustrated by Joe Cepeda

Happy to Be Nappy by bell hooks, illustrated by Chris Raschka

Cornrows by Camille Yarbrough, illustrated by Carole Byard

Bintou's Braids by Sylviane A. Diouf, illustrated by Shane W. Evans

Creating Invitations in Response to Literature Discussions

Students' reading of and response to texts can lead to invitations to contemplate and extend first thoughts and initial impressions. After *Amigos del otro lado/Friends from the Other Side* (Anzaldua 1995) has been read aloud in Room 4, one child wonders where the story takes place; another says, "In Mexico," and supports this assertion by pointing at the pictures. The teacher could have responded by saying, "Let's look in the book and find out," pointing out the usefulness of text in confirming or challenging initial

INVITATION: Magic Windows/Ventanas Mágicas

Elizábeth, Grade 5

When Maria, Nina, Mindy, and Colin were working together last Friday, Maria created a paper cutout. When she shared it with her group, they were reminded of a snowflake, but Maria was thinking of the *papel picado* (cut-paper art whose history stretches back to the early Aztecs) that often are seen as banners stretched across zócalos, plazas, or patios during celebrations in Mexico.

Carmen Lomas Garza has written several books that celebrate her Mexican American history and heritage. Her books about "magic windows," which include history, personal stories, and how-to directions, help us understand more about Maria's thinking and experiences

You're invited to explore some of Carmen Lomas Garza's books and work. After working with your classmates, consider how you can share what you've learned.

Resources
Bilingual Picture Book
Magic Windows/Ventanas Mágicas by Carmen Lomas Garza, Harriet Rohmer, and David Schecter

How-to Instructional Book
Making Magic Windows: Creating Papel Picado/Cut-Paper Art with Carmen Lomas Garza by Carmen Lomas Garza

Website
www.carmenlomasgarza.com/

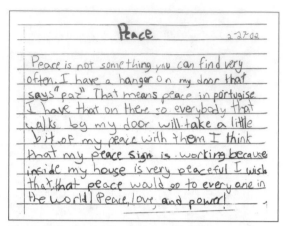

FIGURE 4–11. Andréa's peace writing

assumptions or predictions. Another possible response might be, "Why do the pictures make you think it is Mexico?" The ensuing discussion takes a few initial steps toward investigating how one comes to construct seemingly certain mental images of places, people, or scenarios.

The Images of Mexico invitation (page 64) continues the lines of thinking initiated in this whole-class discussion. It creates space for further thinking about perceptions of places one has never been (though one may have seen images of them in movies and books or on television) and the role classmates who have lived in or visited these places can play in altering those perceptions.

Creating Invitations in Response to Student Art, Dramatizations, or Musical Performances

Student thinking is not only made visible by talking or writing. Students' art can inspire new invitation opportunities as well. Gino's map of his family (Figure 4–3) reveals whom he lives with, plays with, and visits and contradicts the dominant vision of family as a small nuclear unit with one or two parental figures. Building on Gino's drawing and his thinking in relation to it, his teacher could create an invitation (as shown on page 65) to investigate how notions of family are constructed and portrayed.

INVITATION: Peace, Power, and Action

How does one work for a better world?

People protest, flocks fight, kids ask, cows type, coalitions collaborate, and janitors strike. . . .

Andréa put a sign on her door. Other people write books or fold paper cranes. What can you do?

You're invited to read the books listed below to learn more about actions real people and fictional characters have taken.

* Who took action?
* What led up to their decision?
* What risks did they take?
* What do these readings and experiences mean for you and how you live?

Resources
Picture Books
Si, Se Puede/Yes, We Can: Janitor Strike in L.A. by Diana Cohn, illustrated by Francisco Delgado

Sadako by Eleanor Coerr, illustrated by Ronald Himler

Click, Clack, Moo: Cows That Type by Doreen Cronin, illustrated by Betsy Lewin

Feathers and Fools by Mem Fox, illustrated by Nicholas Wilton

Sami and the Time of the Troubles by Florence Perry Heide and Judith Heide Gilliland, illustrated by Ted Lewin

The Day the Earth Was Silent by Michael McGuffee, illustrated by Edward Sullivan

INVITATION: Images of Mexico

Look at the books *Amigos del otro lado/Friends from the Other Side* and *Tomás and the Library Lady*. Where do they take place–the United States or Mexico? Why might some readers respond "Mexico" and others "the United States"?

As readers we bring our experiences to every text that we read. Our experiences help us make predictions and draw conclusions. Sometimes, we need to step back and look at how our experiences are related to our expectations.

What images come to mind when you think about Mexico? Where do these images come from? You're invited to think, read, talk, and explore images of Mexico. What do you notice? Do your ideas about Mexico match or challenge what you see? What surprises you? How might you explain your surprises?

Resources

Poetry
My Mexico/Mexico Mio by Tony Johnston

Picture Books
Amigos del otro lado/Friends from the Other Side by Gloria Anzaldua, edited by Harriet Rohmer, David Schecter, illustrated by C. Mendez.
Tomás and the Library Lady by Pat Mora, illustrated by Raul Colón.

Magazines
National Geographic, "Emerging Mexico," a special issue volume, August 1996
Faces, "Mexico," Cobblestone, December 2000

Photograph

Artifacts

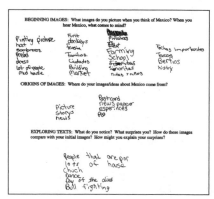

INVITATION: Stories of Family(ies)

Family can mean many things. Families are big. Families are small. Families are close and distant. Families face challenges. Families celebrate. Families move. Families change. . . .

You're invited to think about your definitions, experiences, and stories of family(ies). Read, recite, listen to and/or watch some of others' stories included with this invitation. Use music, art, drama, and/or language as you inquire into family.

What do you notice? Whose stories are told? Whose stories are missing? And why? What other questions come to mind? What do these stories mean to you and the lives of those around you?

Resources
Picture Books
How Tia Lola Came to (Visit) Stay by Julia Alvarez

I Love Saturdays and Domingos by Alma Flor Ada, illustrated by Elina Savadier

Voices in the Park by Anthony Browne

In My Family/En mi familia by Carmen Lomas Garza

When I Am Old with You by Angela Johnson, illustrated by David Soman

Mrs. Katz and Tush by Patricia Polacco

Allison by Allen Say

A Chair for My Mother by Vera B. Williams

Our Gracie Aunt by Jacqueline Woodson, illustrated by Jon Muth

Sweet, Sweet Memory by Jacqueline Woodson, illustrated by Floyd Cooper

Chapter Books
A Step from Heaven by An Na

Becoming Naomi León by Pam Muñoz Ryan

Poetry
Isn't My Name Magical? Sister and Brother Poems by James R. Berry, illustrated by Shelly Hehenberger

The Way a Door Closes by Hope Anita Smith, illustrations by Shane W. Evans

Amber Was Brave, Essie Was Smart by Vera B. Williams

Video
That's a Family by Deborah Chasnoff and Helen S. Cohen

Student	Language(s) Spoken	*What I know about their cultural lives, experiences and resources that they bring to the classroom. . . .*
		• • • • • •
		• • • • • •

FIGURE 4–12. Student information chart

What I've noticed you're interested in and thinking about:

-
-
-
-
-

What have I missed? What are other issues and interests on your mind?

-
-
-
-
-
-

FIGURE 4–13. What's on Your Mind? chart

INVITATION FOR ALL

Collecting Data to Inform Your Teaching and Connect with What's on Your Students' Minds

In order to connect invitations to your students' lives, you need to begin with what you know about them and have learned from them. To what data sources or places can you turn to learn more about your students? Some possibilities are class observations, parent-teacher conferences, and an open-house "interest wall" on which kids and their family members can record graffiti-like questions or issues that are currently on their mind. Come up with some more.

Now think about the students you work with. Then select two students and ponder what you currently know about them. Using the chart in Figure 4–12 (page 66), write in their names and jot down notes on what you currently know about their cultural lives, the resources they bring with them into your classroom, and the issues they face in their day-to-day experiences. Also note the data sources that inform your thinking. (Figure 4–6, on pages 54–56, is an example of a completed chart.) Revisit this chart often as you invite children to undertake activities that foreground their lives: make revisions and additions as you continue to learn about, from, and with your students.

As you reflect on what you know about the two students you selected, consider potential invitations, like My Maps or What's in a Name?, that might allow you to learn more about their interests, experiences, and resources. What invitation themes or issues might appeal to them? What starting points can you imagine that will build on what students know and are open to broad ranges of experiences?

You can also turn to students to learn more about their interests and questions. Create a chart like the one in Figure 4–13 (page 67) and share it with your whole class. Place it where students can add to it as new options surface. Use the chart to help you decide, based on your students' thinking, what invitations would make sense to help this group of students become members of the critical literacy club.

Selecting Supportive Materials

5

In order to invite students to use their social, cultural, and linguistic resources to construct, negotiate, and interrogate meaning, we need to study what our students bring to the curricular table and decide which materials will speak to and extend the issues on our students' minds.

Making Informed Choices

In the invitations discussed so far, students have analyzed newspaper advertisements, gathered data from the Internet, used maps, explored literature, and responded to life events by talking and drawing. All these scenarios involve texts. If texts are defined as message-carrying entities using a specific culturally understood code, then photos, spoken exchanges, a notebook entry written in Hebrew, and so on, are all texts. While schools and classrooms often privilege books, print, and the English language, it is important always to push ourselves to expand the textual resources we both provide and allow students to access as they learn.

There is power in offering a wide range of textual materials so that students can think about themes and issues rather than examine a single book or perspective. Assembling sets of related texts, often referred to as *text sets*, encourages readers to extend their thinking beyond literal comprehension (Crafton 1981; Short, Harste, and Burke 1988). Text sets can prompt readers to make connections with personal experiences, known events, and issues of current concern. Working with multiple texts reveals diverse perspectives, contradictions, and tensions that give students reason to question, inquire into, and reflect on the world and their position in it.

Simply collecting a lot of resources is not enough. We need to discriminate, be intentional about our choices and groupings. In order to open our invitations to a wide range of language users, we need to pay attention to the following considerations:

1. If we want all students to see themselves as active and valued participants, we must select texts that reflect cultural and linguistic diversity.

2. If we want to complicate students' notions of *how it is*, we need to include texts that represent diverse perspectives, purposes, and authorial positions in a range of genres.
3. If we want students to become more than readers of words, we need to incorporate texts that encourage students to become readers of visual images, music, intonation, etc.

Offering Texts That Reflect Linguistic and Cultural Diversity

Culturally relevant texts allow readers to see themselves and their experiences as important potential resources in making meaning (Enciso 1997; Bishop 1997). Such texts must do more than tell others' stories, promote tolerance, or provide information about a cultural group. Culturally relevant texts foreground issues of social representation as they reach beyond notions of heroes and holidays (Nieto 1999) to consider cultural authenticity and authorship (Short and Fox 2003). They invite readers to explore who and what are shaping cultural beliefs. Interacting with culturally and linguistically rich texts calls us, as critically engaged readers, to reflect on our own beliefs and work toward creating a more equitable society.

Consider these examples. In what ways can these students see their experiences as resources for meaning making? In what ways do the texts and how they are positioned push readers to consider the viewpoints of the author(s), their classmates, and others within larger communities, as well as their own?

- Fourth grader Trevor explores his Vietnamese heritage. He wants to find out about more than food, clothing, and celebrations. When a classmate comments that she thinks Vietnam is a war, not a place, the two students have a discussion. Their teacher adds Walter Dean Myers' *Patrol* and Truong Tran's *Going Home, Coming Home* to their collection of resources.
- Missy wonders who decides what constitutes Standard English. Mary argues that everyone should just speak it, because it is how we communicate. As they continue to debate issues of language variety and dialect, they notice that Trish Cooke's *So Much* is published in a dialect different from their spoken language.
- Kelly doesn't see herself as a reader or one traditionally successful in school. Although she's not learning a second language or navigating urban contexts, she *is* experiencing the challenges of rural poverty. Pairing excerpts of Karen Hesse's *Just Juice* with Aliki's *Painted Words, Spoken Memories* complicates notions of becoming literate for both English dominant and new English language learners.
- Shelia is being raised by her grandmother. Alicia constantly tells tales about her grandmother, and echoes her grandmother's beliefs. As they inquire into issues of voice and social stance, Mem Fox's *Wilfred Gorden McDonald Partridge* and Eve Bunting's *The*

Wednesday Surprise complicated these two girls' thinking about the ways in which younger and older generations can both teach and learn from each other.

- Anthony's family structure is shifting. While he lives with a single parent, his classmate Gino lives with many members of his extended family. To these boys it's more than just "having different families." Their lives present different challenges. As part of a Families invitation, they turn to some of Vera Williams' books. These books invite readers to explore stories about family units that differ from the dominant image of a mother, father, and children.

Regardless of the exact titles or texts we choose, we need to assess the diversity of the images we offer and the opportunities our students will have to see themselves and others in the texts they read.

Inviting all students to be critical readers and meaning makers requires that we also offer texts written in languages other than English. Texts may be written completely in Spanish, Hebrew, German, and so on, or include more than one language within a single bi- or multilingual text. Introducing texts written in more than one language places meaning at the center of invitation activity for all learners. When readers can construct meaning in their first language, they are able to contribute richer thinking to the group (Freeman and Freeman 2000; Collier 2004). Multilanguage texts not only make the issues and content associated with an invitation accessible to wider audiences of linguistically diverse readers but also offer students opportunities to study and compare languages. For example, Shelly and Maria read the paired lines of *Hairs/Pelitos* (Cisneros 1997) together, Shelly reading the English text, Maria echoing with the Spanish text. Afterward, talking in English, the two girls related family stories, questioned the ties between hair and culture, and wondered about dominant images of beauty. On another day, two English-dominant students read only the Spanish version of this text in order to test their emergent understanding of Spanish. They discussed grammar and hypothesized meaning based on the words, context, and illustrations. They made linguistic connections between Spanish and English and gained some insights into *how* one learns language.

And while we might not initially consider a book like *The Very Hungry Caterpillar* (Carle 1979, 1992, 1994, 1996a) to address important social issues, offering an invitation with copies of this book in a variety of languages, along with cutout manipulatives of the food consumed by the caterpillar, can lead to important insights and critical thought and action. For example, one day Sara read the Arabic version aloud to her classmates as part of their invitation work. Although her listeners commented that they couldn't understand a word she was saying, they said they understood the story because of the pictures and their previous experiences with the book. Moving on, they discussed directionality of print and what it was like learning new orthographies. English-dominant students caught a glimpse of what it might feel like not to understand a single word and how language learners use a range of cues when constructing meaning. Her classmates were also able to see a new side of Sara—someone who read confidently, who could make sense of Arabic text. As these students continued to talk, Sara explained differences between the printed Arabic she was reading and the dialect spoken by her family. This invitation created space in which an ENL student was able to offer new perspectives for others to contemplate.

Including Texts That Reflect a Variety of Genres, Purposes, and Authorial Perspectives

Poems can celebrate, invite laughter, mourn loss, communicate life-changing experiences, convey scientific information, reflect on the world, and encourage action. Baseball and other trading cards include statistics about teams, players, and characters. Newspaper and magazine editorials critique and question local and global conditions. Feature articles communicate information, persuade, or entertain. Song lyrics, radio broadcasts, and notebook entries relate stories and suggest alternatives. The point is, texts vary—in purpose, content, and design. If we want students to be able to see issues from various points of view, evaluate those points of view, and act accordingly, they need resources that challenge them to think. Locating texts related to our students' interests is not enough; we must also consider *what* information is conveyed and *how* readers engage with the content presented.

One option is to select texts that challenge dominant notions of how the world is or how the world works. As you have probably noticed, many of the invitations in this book use picture books that tell stories that often go untold: the role of women in baseball (*Players in Pigtails*, Corey 2003), the human faces and struggles behind the construction of the transcontinental railroad (*Coolies*, Yin 2003), the realities of Japanese internment in the United States (*The Bracelet*, Ushida 1996), the histories of racial prejudice (*Mississippi Morning*, Vander Zee 2004), and positions surrounding immigration (*Who Belongs Here?* Knight and O'Brien 1996; *Marianthe's Story: Painted Words, Spoken Memories*, Aliki 1998). Texts like these, often referred to as *social issues books* (Harste et al. 2000), make difference visible, voice often-unheard points of view, show how people can take action, help readers question dominant beliefs, and question why certain groups are "othered." Social issues books leave readers thinking, often raising more questions than they answer. While many of the books cited thus far fit the criteria for this genre, they aren't the only options.

We want students to live critically in our classrooms during invitations, independent reading (DEAR, SSR), writing workshop, morning meeting, and so on. We want them to read newspapers and cereal boxes critically at home. We want them to watch the television news with a critical eye. For that to happen, we need to expose them to texts that juxtapose perspectives and invite them to identify and question issues of concern within texts that might not immediately seem to be "about" social issues.

For example, the familiar Berenstain Bears books address issues like the first day of school, new babies, fights, and manners. In *The Berenstain Bears and the Sitter* (Berenstain and Berenstain 1981) Brother and Sister Bear are worried about the arrival of their first baby-sitter, Mrs. Grizzle. However, after they meet Mrs. Grizzle and she shows them her bag of tricks, they find her comforting and fun to spend time with. Readers could find this a helpful, gentle text that relates to their own concerns. They could also question the book's notion of who a baby-sitter is—why isn't the baby-sitter male or young? Readers familiar with *Piggybook* (Browne 1990) might compare what is said and illustrated in that book about being male and female with the Berenstain baby-sitter book. *How* readers engage with these texts is what matters—while the stories may initially resonate with some class members' lived experiences, they can use their thinking as initial steps toward rewriting how the world works.

We also need to think about everyday reading that isn't book oriented. Imagine walking down the cereal aisle at the grocery store and noticing all the options. Stopping to read the Harmony box (a General Mills brand of cereal targeted at women), a critical reader like Steve might ask, "Why is this cereal just for women?" (see Figure 5–1). Another critical reader might recognize that women have different health needs but expand the question to compare claims—nutritionally speaking, how does Harmony compare with cereals marketed for a more general audience, like Kellogg's Smart Start? Discovering that Smart Start contains 100 percent of the recommended daily allowance of iron and Harmony 50 percent, this critical reader might ask new questions about marketing and how it influences what we think we know about health and safety.

While picture books and cereal boxes lend themselves to being read and reread within shorter periods of time, we should not forget the power of poetry or the role of short vignettes or excerpts from larger pieces of literature as we pair potential resources with invitations. We also need to provide the best possible representations of what we currently know about topics and issues—up-to-date information is crucial to authentic inquiry. This means we need to trust our students as developing critical readers and invite them to engage with more texts than those housed in the children's sections of libraries and bookstores.

Invitation resources should reflect our understanding that the world and what we know is constantly changing. Carolyn Burke reminds us that we shouldn't simplify the world for children but rather clarify approximate understanding when need be. So if our students are studying hurricanes and relief efforts and happen to be navigating the latest information on the National Oceanic and Atmospheric Administration's website (http://hurricanes.noaa.gov/), we might need to inquire alongside our students and gain

Reading cereal critically is like how to say things in different ways.
How to find stereotypes. Not just breezing past it. Actually stopping and saying "Why is this cereal just for women?"

FIGURE 5–1. Steve's reflective notes

new understanding ourselves. Then again, students may not need our help, may be able to read quite successfully in the company of their classmates. Gee (2004) writes about learning principles embedded in video games, noting that they are pleasantly frustrating to play and provide information "just in time." Resources accompanying invitations should do the same. If texts are important and meaningful, readers will meet the challenge of reading them when they need the information. The right texts may not be at "grade level." But when readers are motivated by interest, purpose, and need; surrounded with contextual clues; and able to work in a social context in which talk is welcomed, tackling difficult texts becomes just another thing they do.

When exploring immigration, students might look at census data, read or listen to essays by Julia Alvarez (*Something to Declare*, 1999), explore drafts of current legislation, or read Amy Tan's (1990) chapters in *The State of the Language*. For a poetry invitation, poems might just as likely be drawn from *My Man Blue* (Grimes 2002) as from *Another America/Otra America* (Kingsolver 1998) or the Sunday newspaper or a poetry magazine. Elementary readers might be invited to read about how Kingsolver became a poet. We might let students discover the role of "refrigerator notes" in Kingsolver's poetry writing as they listen to her introduction on the audiotape version of *Another America/Otra America*. Inquirers can be invited to read *Time for Kids* articles alongside *Time* or *Utne Reader* articles. By pairing the most current texts we can find with everyday texts (cereal boxes, newspaper columns, letters, comic strips, advertisements, feature articles, radio interviews), familiar stories, and social issues books, we can create text sets that lead readers into complex conversations rather than singular or simple text-tied responses.

A prime example is students' engagement with a Being and Becoming President invitation. Students certainly went beyond the three branches of government, the electoral college, and how a bill becomes a law. As their inquiries unfolded they found articles on polling and spin doctoring, stump speeches, Article II of the Constitution, and a taped radio program featuring Cokie Roberts, President Ford, President Carter, and President George H. W. Bush. These resources were not at their reading level—some were primary documents (Article II of the Constitution and transcripts of interviews), others, newspaper and Internet articles—but that didn't stop them. Together they picked apart paragraphs, digging for information that would help them better understand the politics of being and becoming president. As they struggled to decipher political and legal discourse, these readers gained more than facts: they learned that texts are products of a particular society and are often intended to include or exclude particular readers.

As we assemble poems, vignettes, feature articles, newspaper clippings, nonfiction pieces, directions, and the like, we also need to consider authorship. Within the resources suggested thus far are woven the voices of scientists, journalists, marketers, poets, essayists, and politicians. But we can't forget our voices or the voices of our students. Our own texts can also become part of invitation text sets. As class members take notes, write down their reactions, gather data, and draft personal stories related to an invitation, we should invite them to leave these texts with the invitation. Encountering a textual trail traveled by past participants gives newcomers to the invitation additional perspectives and options as they chart their own invitation pathways.

The Images of Mexico invitation is another example. When this invitation was first offered, the folder included two picture books, two magazines containing Mexico-related articles, teacher-taken photographs, and a letter written by a Mexican student sharing her perspectives on life in Mexico. However, as the invitation participants came and went, they made lists of their preconceived notions of Mexican life as well as possible sources of these images they associated with Mexican culture (movies, postcards, travel ads, news reports, etc.). These texts (see Figure 5–2) and others then became part of the invitation.

FIGURE 5–2. Ana Cristina's notes

Choosing Texts That Move Beyond Words and Encourage Many Ways of Knowing

Written language is often privileged as *the* sign system for making meaning. Selecting texts that invite students to make meaning using music, movement, art, and math expands potential learning. Therefore, we explicitly need to select texts that use art, music, movement, and design to communicate meaning. Consider these scenarios:

- *Images of Mexico*: Four girls pour over a foldout photograph of Mexico City in the August 1996 issue of *National Geographic* as they discuss the differences and similarities between pueblo life and life with their *abuelos* in the city. They have selected this text from the options in the invitation's folder. The other visual texts in the folder include photographs taken and postcards collected by the students and teacher while living or traveling in Mexico. (Other potential sources of visual texts include coffee-table books on Mexico, printouts of Internet pictures, newspaper clippings, travel ads, calendar pages, etc.)
- *Natural Disaster Relief*: A second grader begins perusing Internet sites to track current hurricane activity and cleanup efforts. When he discovers video images of tornadoes and hurricanes, he begins to record his journey cutting, pasting, and organizing images using PowerPoint (see Figure 5–3). This student has located visual texts related to his questions. He is not only reading visual images but

FIGURE 5–3. Sample slide from Caleb's PowerPoint using visual literacies

also using them to produce new texts. PowerPoint allows him to design images that sort out his findings and communicate his learning experiences to others.

- *Music, Music Everywhere*: Three students are reading musical song cards. (Music cards indicate note sequences without rhythmic notations.) After taking turns practicing, they perform, for the class, a series of simple songs on an electric piano. Nina, who is from Israel, correctly plays the notes for "Baa, Baa, Black Sheep," but her listeners tell her the tune isn't "right," because she is using a Middle Eastern rhythm. Her performance invites dialogue, prompts questions, and challenges students' notions about "just knowing how a song goes." They begin to see knowledge as a product of cultural experience.

- *Why Is It Written Like This?* Two girls study a box of cereal. They note nutritional claims and the font size and position of two advertisements: "free baseball cards inside" and "free CD offer." They know that this particular box of cereal did not contain the free baseball cards. They begin to write down things they want to say when they call the cereal company's offices. These students are decoding language, but they're also using design to inform their thinking. Is a big yellow sunburst proclaiming free baseball cards speaking to parents purchasing cereal? Are the nutritional claims accurate? Why is bigger print used for the "free stuff," while the nutritional information is in tiny print? As these girls prepare and rehearse an oral response, they're doing much more than decoding and encoding language. They're reading designs, questioning what texts are accomplishing, and using their literacy to take action.

- *I See the Rhythm*: Invitations can include sound as well as visual images. Two boys look at a time line in *I See the Rhythm* (Igus and Wood 1998) as they listen to pieces by some of the artists featured in the book. They alternate between reading the narrative, listening to CD tracks, looking at the book's artwork, and examining the time lines. After gathering information from the book and CD tracks, which include Charles Brown and Eddie Williams' "Driftin' Blues," Duke Ellington's "Cotton Tail," and Charlie Parker and Dizzie Gillespie's performance of "Leap Frog," participants compose their own works of art in response to the music.

- We might create an invitation that brings together Paul Fleishman's book *Rondo in C* (1998), an audio recording of *Rondo in C*, and an orchestral score of the piece. Or we might invite students to explore the connections between song, social critique, and action using a music video such as Sarah McLachlan's *World on Fire* (www.worldonfire.ca/).

- We could design invitations that pair books like *Lookin' for Bird in the Big City* (Burleigh 2001) and jazz recordings; locate music composed or written for social action; bring together texts that capture song and dance on paper (*I See a Song* by Eric Carle [1996b], *Song and Dance Man* by Karen Ackerman [1992], *Rap a Tap Tap* by Leo Dillon and Diane Dillon [2002]); or highlight women singers (*Ella Fitzgerald* by Andrea Pinkney [2002], and *When Marian Sang* by Pam Muñoz Ryan [2002]).

The options are infinite, but we must not forget the role of our students' experiences, questions, and wondering when constructing such invitations.

Moving Beyond Linear Readings and Predicable Responses

Invitations are not just about the quantity of texts or ideas. Rich texts sets are a great step forward, but they are just the beginning. How we use texts is equally important. We need to use texts that honor the properties of invitations, invite reading across and between texts, and prompt critical questions and responses. How did the readers in the previous examples use texts?

Invitation participants do not always read line by line, page by page. In *Images of Mexico*, they started paging through an issue of *National Geographic* and were stopped by the foldout photo of Mexico City. In *Why Is It Written Like This?* the girls gravitated toward the sunburst advertising free baseball cards in large type. In *Natural Disaster Relief*, Caleb began to investigate live storms instead of relief efforts—this is the beauty of invitations, being able to take an angle that matches your questions. Keeping in mind that not every last word or image needs to be examined, we also might choose more books, like *My Map Book* (Fanelli 1995) and *The National Civil Rights Museum Celebrates Everyday People* (Duncan and Smith 1996), that contain multiple points of entry and allow readers to wander through them making connections and locating information of interest. When creating invitations we might also use sticky notes to draw readers' attention to particular sections of texts. For example, we might choose a vignette or two from Cisnero's memoirlike *The House on Mango Street* (1991), the introduction to Naomi Shihab Nye's *The Flag of Childhood: Poems from the Middle East* (2002), and particular photos in Peter Menzel's *Material World* (1995).

Another way we can support the development of critical reading practices is to help readers see that a text is not a product of a single author's thinking or imagination. This may mean that we need to include background on authors and reviews of their works. For example, as kids find out about Eve Bunting's immigrant experience and her belief that kids tackle difficult issues every day, they might think differently about why she wrote *Smokey Night* (1999), *Going Home* (1998), or *A Day's Work* (1997). They might wonder what lenses, information sources, and experiences Eve Bunting uses to view, understand, and reconstruct events. Similarly, they might question how David Diaz's or Ronald Himler's illustrations impact readers' interactions with these books. If they look at other texts they have illustrated, they might hypothesize about how these illustrators decide which books match their artistic and social interests. We might also call attention to forewords or afterwords. Information shared by Pam Muñoz Ryan in her afterword to *When Marian Sang* identifies the story as nonfiction and points up a lesser-known part of our history. The final pages of *Ellington Was Not a Street* (Shange 2004) share further insight into the lives of influential twentieth-century African Americans like Ellington, Du Bois, Paul Robeson, and others—the amount of information is just enough to evoke more questions and launch continued inquiries. We might also pair books like *The Great Migration* (Lawrence 1993), which features a series of paintings by Jacob Lawrence, with *Story Painter* (Duggleby 1989), which details Lawrence's artistic agenda. Or we might bring together Langston Hughes' poem "The Negro Speaks of Rivers" with a book like *Langston's Train Ride* by Robert Burleigh (2004), that frames the larger story surrounding the writing of the poem. Added information complicates interpretations and helps readers discover the social purposes texts can serve. Calling attention to why authors write or painters paint encourages readers to reach beyond the text and consider how they might act differently as a result of thinking about these resources and the men and women who created them.

Classroom practices often emphasize personal and text-based connections. Critically engaged readers move beyond personal and text-to-text connections. For example, as three boys inquire into immigration, they discover that one of their classmates, Arvin, is considered an immigrant. Their conversation doesn't stop there. Together the boys then read a newspaper article about the current politics of immigration. As they learn more, they weigh their classmate's position and experiences against the thinking expressed in the article and begin to articulate their stance. As critical readers their talk didn't stop with the connection between immigrants in general and Arvin's experiences. Rather, Arvin's experiences repositioned immigration as a contemporary rather than historical issue. Wanting to know how and if immigrants' experiences have changed over time, they moved to broader social contexts and read with social purpose. These critical readers are code breakers. They are also readers who use the texts before them to construct personal meanings, but together their interactions lead them to "talk back" to an issue of larger social concern—namely, that it isn't as easy as it might look to live the "American Dream."

Selecting rich texts that are culturally relevant and value many ways of knowing encourages critical engagement, but critical engagement also depends on the experience readers have reading critically. For help crafting questions that prompt critical engagement, we can turn to the four dimensions of critical literacy (refer back to Figure 2–3): disrupting commonplace notions of how life is, considering multiple viewpoints, connecting thinking and interpretations to larger social structures, and taking informed action.

For example, students working with The Right to Read invitation might be offered two initiating texts: *Richard Wright and the Library Card* (Miller 1999) and a section of Richard Wright's 1945 autobiography *Black Boy* (1998). Initiating questions could be generated for each dimension:

Disrupting the Commonplace

- What are Miller's intentions when he decides to fictionalize some of Wright's experiences (for example, the librarian who laughs when Wright pretends to be illiterate)?
- What underlying messages do these texts convey?

Considering Multiple Viewpoints

- Whose voices are missing in Miller's book? In Wright's autobiography?
- How else could the picture-book version be written?

Focusing on the Sociopolitical

- How are Wright's experiences related to larger cultural stories of today?
- Who has power? Is it foregrounded? Hidden?

Taking Action

- How is language used to question or resist injustice?
- Who could have allied with Wright and taken action with him?
- How does this story affect how we live today?

The four dimensions framework is not only helpful in angling how texts can be used, but can also be a useful tool for choosing the texts. Examining several dimensions of texts pushes us to think through the many possible reading experiences that can transpire between readers and texts. Looking at my library shelves, I might decide that *Going North* (Harrington 2004), a book about a family moving from Alabama through the segregated South to Nebraska in the 1960s, is a book that disrupts the commonplace in the way it challenges dominant and historical definitions of what it means to be a pioneer. Titles that could be thought of as resources that encourage the consideration of multiple viewpoints include *We Were There, Too! Young People in U.S. History* (Hoose 2001), *From Wall to Wall* (Kuklin 2002), and *Voices in the Park* (Browne 2001). Books like *If the World Were a Village* (Smith 2002) situate thinking in larger contexts and *Duck for President* (Cronin 2004) foreground issues of power. Lastly, titles such as Toni Morisson's *Remember: The Journey to School Integration* (2004), *¡Si, Se Puede!/Yes We Can* (Cohn 2002), and *Harvesting Hope: The Story of Cesar Chavez* (Krull 2003) share stories of social action as the Little Rock Nine, L.A. janitors, and the United Farm Workers collectively worked for change. While many of the resources suggested thus far in this book could be categorized in multiple dimensions, the act of sorting resources by dimension isn't about determining "correct" classifications; rather it's a way of thinking through the range of resources students can access.

INVITATION FOR ALL

Designing Invitations for Your Teaching Context

You've read a number of invitations, begun to develop an image of what they look like, and learned about where these invitations took some of the students in Room 4. You've started making lists of what you know about your students and the issues on their minds and explored many ways of selecting and using diverse resources.

Now write some invitations appropriate for your own teaching. What's an issue on your students' minds? What resources do you know or can you locate that speak to these issues? Select the focal issue.

Begin to assemble potential resources. In pulling together material consider cultural and linguistic diversity, varied genres, and a wide range of authors. Think about how your emerging text set reflects and encourages many ways of knowing. Use Figure 5–4 and the four dimensions framework

---

Checklist to Support Diverse Text Selection

As you think about the invitations being offered in your classroom, do they include:

____ Texts written in languages other than English?
____ Multilingual texts?
____ Accurate representations of diverse cultural experiences and contexts?
____ A wide range of genres?
____ Poems? Advertisements? Song lyrics?
____ Nonfiction resources (photo essays, textbook selections, biographies, picture books, scholarly texts, etc.)?
____ Contemporary and historical texts?
____ Photographs?
____ Newspaper, magazine, and/or Internet articles?
____ Works of art (reproductions of paintings, sketches, sculptures, tapestries, murals, artifacts, etc.)?
____ CD or video recordings of music, dramatic performances, documentaries, interviews, and/or media portrayals of current events?
____ Texts authored by outside experts, publishers, teachers, family members, and students?

FIGURE 5–4. Checklist for supporting diverse, supportive materials

to examine the resources you gather. Look back to the properties to consider how texts are positioned and might be used by teachers and students alike.

Frame an initiating experience and invitation. Generate suggested questions. Invite your students to try out your new invitation and see where they go! You might inquire alongside them, take notes and study what goes well and what teaching interactions might be needed, or observe paths taken as various groups work with the same invitation.

6 Teaching Inquiry Through Strategy Lessons

So far, you've seen invitations in action as students have critically studied and redesigned Mother's Day ads, questioned currency and colonialism, and explored mapping as a window into one another's lives and a means for reflection. You know that critical curricular invitations prompt participants to make decisions about the issues with which they engage, the questions they ask, the company in which they learn, and the activity in which they participate. You know that resources matter and that invitations require spaces and processes that enable all participants to be meaning makers, inquirers, critics, and activists. Critical curricular invitations are opportunities for powerful learning fueled by powerful teaching.

Our students learn from every move we, as teachers, make—we're always teaching *something*. When we're observing student activity, we're teaching that process matters. When we respond to minipresentations with genuine questions, we're teaching response techniques as well as demonstrating that we too are learners. When we introduce texts that complicate issues, we're teaching that multiple perspectives are important. These teaching moves may be subtle, but they're essential.

However, at times our teaching may need to be more explicit in order to help invitation participants further develop what they know about being a critical inquirer. Our teaching can help make students aware of their current actions, help them develop more critical practices, and/or expand students' ways of reading, responding, and reacting to issues of local and global concern.

Becoming a Critical Inquirer

Students' work in the classroom is based on their current understanding and previous experiences. In other words, if students' previous research experiences have focused on dates of birth, time lines, and retellings of events, these are the kinds of things they're likely to "find out" about someone or something. If our invitations are to challenge, stretch, and encourage students to use literacy to understand and transform themselves and the world, we need to help students move beyond fact finding, retelling, and making personal connections and use the issues they explore as a way to create a more just world.

Critical inquirers pay attention to the world. They ask questions, wonder about how the world is and how it could be. Their work embraces tensions as they move toward new understanding. They follow Freire's (1985) advice and not only work to solve problems but pose problems for further thought and consideration. Their work often generates more questions than answers: as fifth grader Brian states, "How can you know what you want to know until you know more about it?" Inquirers see their work as ongoing: inquirers have stamina and perseverance. They may reach points within inquiries at which it makes sense to stop or wrap up their current thinking, but destinations are rarely finite.

Creating Classrooms for Authors and Inquirers (Short, Harste, and Burke 1996) supports Brian's thinking that in true inquiry we often dedicate more time to figuring out and revising our questions than seeking "answers." In classrooms and learning contexts in which students are invited to be inquirers, learning begins with what students know. Students are given the time, tools, and resources they need to generate questions. Inquiry questions are genuine—they're not questions students are *supposed* to ask or angled toward predetermined outcomes learners *should* discover. Inquirers explore issues, try out and reflect on new insights and understanding, in safe spaces; they're not always expected to *get it right*. Inquiry embraces approximations and process. Inquiry is a perspective toward learning (and thus a perspective toward teaching).

Seeing, Valuing, and Teaching Processes for Critical Inquiry

Angling teaching toward supporting our students' growth as active, critical inquirers requires valuing not only *what, when,* and *where* learners learn but also *how* learning takes place. We need to help our students become aware of and refine their learning processes. Becoming aware of *what, when, where,* and *how* learners learn depends on how we understand each of these words and what we see as potential sources of information (presentations, artifacts, reflections, and so on). So that we're all on the same page, I'm using *what* to refer to content, *how* to refer to process and practices, and *when* and *where* to refer to configurations and/or structures that might support learning.

If we were to ask students to talk about their learning, they would, depending on their experiences as learners, likely tell us *what* they were learning about and/or *when* they were engaged in particular learning activities ("during math we were doing fractions"; "while reading a *National Geographic* magazine, I learned about the size of Mexico City"). Shifting their awareness to processes and practices is challenging yet important. Processes and practices can last a lifetime; specific content, classes, or locations do not. Helping kids become aware of their moves and decisions as they pose problems and explore possible solutions helps them live critically beyond our watch.

Shifting what we look for, both during invitation work and in the classroom in general, is much like the shift writers make when they move from reading like readers to reading like writers, discovering how they might structure text and/or powerfully use words within their own work. Katie Wood Ray (1999) uses the metaphor of looking at a dress. A shopper wanting to purchase one might be concerned with color or size. A seamstress intending to make a similar dress might look at fabric, seams, cuts, lengths, and so forth. Ralph Fletcher (2000) uses the metaphor of how fans, coaches, and parents of players might watch a soccer game: fans are concerned with the team as a whole, coaches zero in on the intricate interactions of every play, and parents focus on a particular player. These metaphors also ask us to look beyond artifacts, like dresses or written soccer plays, to human actions and interactions. As teachers and experienced kidwatchers (Goodman 1985), we may already attend to students' activity as if we're coaches or study artifacts like seamstresses, but we need to invite our students to join us. Our students need to become researchers who study their own learning lives as well as the lives of those with whom they learn. We need to start conversations with our students about what it means to shift from thinking, "I'm learning about world currency," to "When I was looking at coins, I started to wonder why the queen of England was on lots of them. So now I'm looking at more information about currency to see what I can find out." Students need to be coresearchers and coteachers who are skilled in attending to, thinking about, and talking about process as well as content.

We teach process and possible practices when we invite students to participate in whole- or small-group reflective *strategy lessons* or *in-the-moment teaching interactions*. Keeping in mind that *doing* and *participating* is central to learners' growth, we want to be conscious of how much time we spend on explicit teaching. For example, if we call students together for a strategy lesson on how groups incorporate all members, we want to keep our teaching brief and centered. I hesitate to place time limits on strategy lessons or in-the-moment teaching interactions, because I've seen valuable learning stem from two-minute interactions and twenty-minute conversations. However, talking about everything that groups could do can be overwhelming. Keeping teaching brief and focused and ensuring that students have opportunities to *do* what we're teaching are what's important.

What we teach should be anchored in our observations of what students need. Knowing that we want our teaching to be long-lasting and that we can't teach everything in one day, it seems smart to observe groups' actions for a while before joining in or interrupting. As we watch, we can ask ourselves questions to help us decide what we will teach, to whom, and how:

- Are similar needs or patterns of activity evident in several groups or the whole class?
- Will naming what students are doing help them in their current or future practices?

- Are there strategies or suggestions that will expand the practices students are currently using?
- Is there something that could be demonstrated as a new option for inquirers?

Teaching Critical Inquiry Practices

When students begin working with invitations, they need images of what this work looks like. To help students see possibilities for processes and practices, you can teach small- and whole-group strategy lessons. Unlike reading and writing workshops, where almost every day opens with a minilesson, invitation strategy lessons are less frequent and offered based on class needs.

Teaching Observation

Observation heightens students' awareness of the work an invitation entails and points them toward more (and more precise) interactions. Just as they might watch fish swimming in a bowl, class members gather around and observe a group of students positioned in the center of the room, working together on an invitation for an uninterrupted period. The observers take notes (perhaps on blank overhead transparencies) and discuss what they've noticed after the group has finished. Alternatively, you may "pause" the action periodically and let the class discuss particular moves and decisions. A fishbowl not only allows students to see what is possible but also helps students talk about future options relative to their role and involvement in invitations.

Depending on your purpose, those watching might take notes on:

- Who participates.
- How turns are taken.
- What sorts of questions are asked.
- What participants do once questions are raised.
- How participants keep the inquiry going.
- How plans are made and actions taken.

In the following example, some of the students in Room 4 are watching Shelly and Maria work on the Hair invitation (see pages 59–60), focusing on the ways in which Shelly and Maria interact as they negotiate and carry out their plans. It is a Wednesday in late January, a year and a half into Maria's experiences as an English language learner. The two girls are sitting at a table near the window. They have the two-pocket folder containing the formal invitation; the children's literature listed on it; printouts from websites in which these authors talk about their writing interests and intentions; a photograph of a little Filipino girl entering a beauty salon with a hairstyle poster displayed close to the entryway; and writings and drawings of their classmates who have already worked on this invitation.

Opening the folder, Shelly tells Maria that this invitation is about hair. The two girls leaf through the books and resources, and then Shelly starts reading the cover page to Maria. After considering possible starting points, Shelly suggests beginning with *Hairs/Pelitos*. They agree on the book and begin reading it. Shelly reads in English to Maria, Maria reads in Spanish to Shelly. Next, they read *I Love My Hair!* and some notes from its author Natasha Anastasia Tarpley's website. They pause often, clarifying concepts like *tangles*, telling stories of having their hair braided or cut, making intertextual connections, and asking questions. As they move from book to book, they wonder, "Why is hair different?" They write this question down and move on.

Looking at the photograph, Maria points out, "That poster, that poster, there are more people with hair that's not like her. The girl, she's different from—," her way of saying that little girl in the photo and the women in the hairstyle poster don't share the same cultural background. Maria says she's seen similar hairstyle posters in Mexico and adds, "Mine's not like that," meaning that her dark, thick hair is not like that of the seemingly white women in the poster. Continuing to think aloud she muses, "Maybe her mom or dad is like that."

Shelly goes back to Tarpley's notes, pages through *Wild, Wild Hair* (Grimes 1997), and shares her thinking, "I wonder what, if I can say this right. The little girl's hair is like [classmate] Fernanda's hair. I got it, but I don't know how to say it. That's not like her natural heritage, to have hair like that, to be white. [The women in the poster] should be like, from there, the Philippines. Like hair describes where she's from, hair describes their culture, maybe they're advertising hairdos but why like this? So hair is like, it's like cultural heritage, but this poster is not [the little girl's]. Why not? I'll write that. And we can ask."

Afterward, the group of students observing Shelly and Maria's work make a chart of what invitation activity might *look*, *sound*, and *feel like* (see Figure 6–1) and share their observations with the whole class. The student presenters talk about how the girls explain things to each other, make notes for themselves as well as their presentation, share reading responsibilities, use both Spanish and English, and explore other perspectives as they use the visual and print-based materials. Class members suggest additions to the chart based on their experiences that day, and the chart is then hung on the classroom wall to remind students of possible ways they might engage in future work.

Mapping Paths of Inquiry

Mapping paths taken by various groups of invitation inquirers is another strategy aimed at increasing students' attention to inquiry processes. How you map students' activity and/or create the maps (on chart paper, on blank overheads, with computer software, etc.) depends on your teaching intentions. You can collect student-created maps over time and position them together for comparative purposes. Or you might create a map yourself using the notes you've taken watching a particular group. You might sit down with

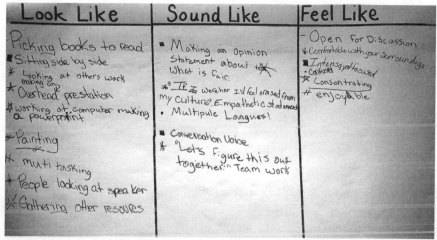

Look Like	Sound Like	Feel Like
Picking books to read ■ Sitting side by side * Looking at others work making an * Overhead prestation # working at computer making a powerprirint * Painting * multi tasking * People looking at speaker * Gathering other resources	■ Making an opinion Statement about what is fair * "If I wereher I'd feel erased from my culture. Empathetic statement • Multiple Langues! ■ Converseation Voice * "Let's figure this out together." Team work	- Open for Discussion * Comfortable with your surroundings ■ Intensy/focused • Confused * Consontrating # enjoyable

FIGURE 6–1. Student-generated chart in response to observing Hair invitation

a small group of students and together reconstruct their work (or a portion of their work) on a given day. Or you can ask students (either in small groups or individually) to map their group's work. Making the maps helps students become aware of their inquiry and learning processes. Using the maps as examples when teaching small groups or the whole class refines students' understanding about possible decisions inquirers make and actions they take.

If you've noticed that some of your students need more support in how to initiate invitations work, you might decide to watch one group's beginning strategies and then help the group prepare a map that lets them *see* their decisions. For example, watching Shelly (a native-English-speaking fifth grader), Nina (a native Hebrew-speaking fourth grader), and Ana Cristina (a native-Spanish-speaking sixth grader) work on the *Memories invitation*, shown on the following page, you take the following notes:

The 3 girls gather around a table with the invitation and books. Nina, who is working with this invitation for a second time, takes the books out of the folder.

Nina begins by saying, "Me no like this [the book *Wilfred Gorden McDonald Partridge*]. Read first, then paint. I want to read. She picks up *Marianthe's Story: Painted Words, Spoken Memories.*

Ana Cristina slides her chair back from the table and distances herself from the book, indicating she is not interested in reading. Nina opens Aliki's book and begins to read, pausing when she encounters *Marianthe*, the main character's name.

"This name?" Nina asks Shelly.

"Marianne," Shelly approximates, and Nina continues reading aloud.

While Nina reads, Ana Cristina opens her container of pomegranate seeds and begins to eat her snack as she listens. Nina continues her persistent questioning, wondering "What teammate?" after she encounters the word *teammate* in the picture book. Shelly tries explaining, "It is like someone who is on the team." Nina's tentative "From the team?" suggests she is still unclear. Shelly doesn't respond. Ana Cristina starts talking about football/futból teams (American football and Spanish soccer), baseball teams, and basketball teams. Their talk then turns to Ana Cristina's snack. Noticing that Ana Cristina is eating pomegranate seeds, Nina want to know where she got them. Shelly wants to know what they are. Ana Cristina wants the others to try them. Nina remembers eating pomegranates in Israel and wanting to find them here in the United States.

Making a map of the opening minutes of their work, the three girls and you note that Nina gets the group going. She looks in the folder, picks one book, and then the students start reading together. While no one directly announces the group members are going to take turns reading, passing the book communicates that they are going to share reading responsibilities. As they read, they often pause to "say something" and it isn't always talk just about the book. They take the time to discuss their own experiences and questions, setting the book down as they talk about teams, teammates, football/futból/soccer, and pomegranate seeds. The complete map of their activity is shown in Figure 6-2.

The first time Nina worked with the memories invitation, her classmate Mary had read *Wilfred Gordon McDonald Partridge* to the group. Then Trevor suggested that each group member paint an intergenerational memory. After everyone had finished, the group started crafting text similar to that in *Wilfred Gordon McDonald Partridge*.

During her second encounter with the invitation, Nina drew on her earlier experiences in several ways. First, she was familiar

FIGURE 6-2. Map of Memories invitation activity

with the books and knew what she didn't want to do. She stated that she didn't like *Wilfred Gordon McDonald Partridge* and chose to begin with the other book. Second, she, like Mary, started the group's work by reading a book. However, unlike Mary, she shared reading responsibilities with her classmates and moved beyond a cover-to-cover read as she, Ana Cristina, and Shelly talked often and at length about an array of topics.

Examining the map during a whole-class strategy lesson, you could have students focus on the group's early activity (points 1 through 6 on the map). One possible teaching point relates to how learners can use past experiences and processes to get invitation work started. Another option might be to draw students' attention to how this group generated and dealt with questions (points 3, 5, 6). Your teaching might highlight the ways learners "find" questions as they move through an activity, thus confirming Brian's earlier thinking that we don't always know at the outset of our inquiries what we need or want to know more about: we need to dig in first. It's safe to say that Shelly, Nina, and Ana Cristina would not have framed questions about cross-cultural sports, how climate influences available fruits, and/or the challenges of reading printed English before they had read Aliki's book.

Another teaching possibility is to construct another map based on Shelly and Maria's work on the Hairs invitation (see Figure 6-3) and place it alongside this one. Your teaching could then be angled toward the roles of texts, talk, and questioning in group inquiry. Looked at together, the two maps reveal that each group read, stopped, talked, and questioned throughout their work. You could ask students what they notice about the differences or similarities between how the two groups used texts. The Memories group leaned heavily on the reading of one text, produced spoken and

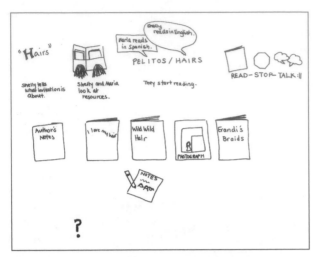

FIGURE 6–3. Map of Hair invitation activity

painted responses, and used their lived experiences to construct new understanding. The Hair group interacted with text in similar ways but used a larger collection of texts, including author's notes from the Internet and a photograph, and their notes included both words and pictures.

Maps allow students to compare, contrast, and learn from one another's processes in thinking about future practices and actions. While there are numerous teaching possibilities, what you choose to highlight should match what you think your students will benefit from given their needs and experiences as inquirers.

Sorting Questions and Responses

Sometimes you'll want to focus on specific practices, like the kinds of questions and responses students are asking and exploring. What types of questions generate rich critical discussion, contemplation, and debate? What content or clarification questions are needed? What types of questions and responses are needed to move groups forward?

Particular types of questions surface again and again during invitation work. At various points in their inquiry, invitation participants ask data-gathering questions, process questions, and critical questions (see Figure 6–4). To help students see the types of questions that they might consider as they work, you could begin a strategy lesson by identifying these categories and giving examples of actual questions students have raised while working on an invitation. Asking students to sort the questions into the three categories helps them think about what each type of question might sound like, as well as when particular types of questions are helpful.

Look at these three questions students asked in the earlier, Memories invitation example:

1. Nina wondered, "This name?" when she read *Marianthe* in the text.
2. After she read the main character's comments about the English alphabet looking like chicken's feet and camel humps, Shelly asked Nina and Ana Cristina about their language-learning experiences: "Was it like that for you?"
3. As they were painting their own memories, Ana Cristina followed up on Nina's comment about access to and conservation of water in Israel: "Not very much water? Why?"

Data-gathering questions	Participants asked *data-gathering questions* when they were interested in:	
	• Learning about others' actions, experiences, and the world	What did you just say? Do? What did you do in school in Algeria? What is your family's hair like? Isn't Day of the Dead like Halloween?
	• Clarifying understandings	This name? What teammate? (from Memories example in this chapter) How do you say _____ in Arabic? Korean? Spanish? English? What's that called?
	• Seeking additional information or resources related to topic or subject	Does anybody have a book about _____? Why are houses made from mud? Is Mexico part of the United States? Where can we find out? Where does it say _____?
Process questions	Participants asked *process questions* when they were interested in:	
	• Moving group activity forward	Trevor? Who's next? Does anybody else have something to say? Do you want to record what we're saying?
	• Facilitating group planning	Are you going to make another one? So now what are we going to do? Do you think we should read this? Who wants to take notes?

FIGURE 6–4. Questioning chart (*continues*)

Critical questions	Participants asked *critical questions* when they were interested in:	
	• Disrupting the commonplace	Why do a lot of people move or immigrate? Why *can't* girls…?
	• Considering multiple viewpoints	What do you think? What's your opinion? Why did the author write this? What would _____ (from specific others to groups like U.N. members, etc.) think?
	• Questioning socio-political contexts	Why is it written like this? Who decides what is proper? Why is it like this? Who benefits from it being this way?
	• Taking action	What should we do? Who wants to be part of the committee?

FIGURE 6–4. *Continued*

Question 1 is a data-gathering question aimed at clarifying understanding. Question 2 is also a data-gathering question but is angled toward gathering information from others' lived experiences. Question 3 is more critical in nature.

Placing questions in particular categories and tallying them up is not the sole purpose here. Strategy lessons are intended to support the taking on of new practices. They can be designed and taught in order to help students understand where and why participants need to ask clarification-type questions. Or, if it seems students are reading books cover to cover without thinking about how they relate to their lives and experiences, a strategy lesson might discuss how and why questions like number 2 further invitation work by positioning classmates' lived experiences as potential learning resources. Or, if students seem experienced and comfortable exploring their own experiences, lessons could focus on moving students toward more critical pursuits (such as question 3). Strategy lessons might also attend to the absence of particular types of questions. For example, the Memories group raised relatively few process questions. Why might this be? What did this group of inquirers know about initiating and engaging in invitation inquiry? What might classmates learn from their understanding?

Sorting is a useful strategy to help students construct their own understanding of what is happening and/or not yet happening. Collect a wide range of questions from a number of invitation groups and record the questions on individual sticky notes or note cards, which can be easily manipulated. Students in Room 4 did this with questions raised during various groups' experiences with the Memories invitation (see Figure 6–5). As students sorted, they had lively debates. Is a question like "What does teammate mean?" purely a definition question? Does a dictionary define every way in which people use the word? They created categories and revised headings that didn't work. At what point a question like "What should we do?" was raised mattered to the students. They needed to differentiate how groups initiated invitation work and when and how they started to sift through their processes and progress to think about how they might present what they discovered to the class. Sorting talk is teaching talk.

How participants respond to one another also makes a difference. Responses determine what questions and practices are valued. Responses determine what sorts of questions are asked again. And responses communicate who matters. Response can be addressed in terms of form, function, and patterns of interaction.

Response is especially important when you invite students to think about, question, and respond to experiences in languages and meaning systems other than spoken or written Standard English. Consider all the scenes you've read so far that include new English language learners. At times their

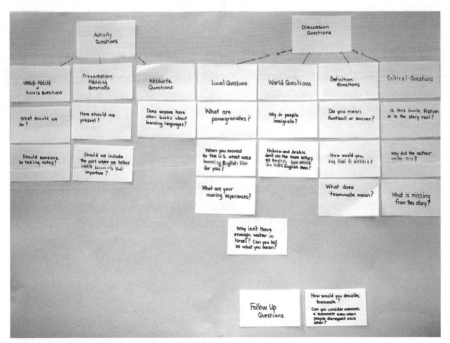

FIGURE 6–5. Student-generated question sort

spoken or written contributions are brief, and their contributions include approximations of Standard English grammar. However, if form is always valued over function, students stop asking questions, responding, or participating (Brock, Parks, and Moore 2004; Wheeler and Swords 2004). In other words, if an ENL or English-dominant child is reading aloud or trying to talk out their thinking and group members constantly interrupt to correct pronunciation, the message being sent is that this reader/thinker isn't reading and/or communicating *correctly* in this performance context. And more than likely in such a scenario the student shifts her attention to saying words rather than meaning. Similarly, if participants are required to frame questions or sentences in a complete, grammatical form aligned with Standard English, these stipulations may distance some participants from active engagement. In other words, responses have the power to both silence and invite further participation.

Students in Room 4 were expected to work collaboratively, be keenly aware of one another's lives, value the processes in which they were engaged, be open to considering alternatives, take risks, and attend to meanings constructed through diverse ways of knowing. These expectations influenced their interactions, including how they responded to their teachers and their peers. Figure 6–6 lists productive ways students in Room 4 responded to one another. This list is not exhaustive; there are many other options. It is, however, a lens through which to observe and reshape interactions in your classroom. You may want to invite students to sort some of their responses to one another in the same way they sorted questions. Use the categories in Figure 6–6, or ask students to generate categories based on what they see happening around them.

Sorting is often the first step in a series of strategy lessons. As students sort, you might also ask them to look for occasions that offer new directions for inquiry. Inviting students to revisit or reexamine the types of questions raised and responses offered will expand the ways in which they interact. For example, there was no response to Ana Cristina's question "Not very much water?"; Shelly's comments about her painting and Christmas memories steered the conversation in another direction. I'm not suggesting that the girls should necessarily have pursued this question, only that it was another option—one that might have angled their work toward social issues associated with water conservation and access to potable water. Co-constructed charts could be used as springboards to think about what future critical questions might sound like and/or what participants might do in response to such queries.

Imagining Alternative Scenarios

You need to be careful not to paint too narrow a picture of what successful invitation activity looks like. Asking equal numbers of the various types of questions doesn't guarantee success. Reading, painting, and presenting aren't *the* right way to engage with the Memories invitation. When you present examples, you need to make sure you also discuss and assess alternatives. Highlighting productive examples encourages students to take risks,

Potential Response	*Response description*
Provide information	• Sharing additional data or perspectives Respondents can use their lives and/or offer textual resources to elaborate on group members' understandings
Make connections	• Linking issues at hand with other related issues Respondents may make connections to their own lives, classmates' lives, other curricular venues, or surrounding social worlds. They may do so using language like: "Gino said that . . ., well what I don't understand then is . . . because it's not what he was thinking when we were talking during morning meeting."
Invite clarification	• Asking participants to elaborate on their thinking, understandings, or position Respondents may use language like: "Say more about that" or "Amber, I still don't understand what you're saying. Can you explain it again?"
Expand participation	• Inviting unheard voices or less active participants to engage more actively in group inquiry Respondents may use language like: "Fernanda hasn't said what she thinks yet" and "Let Nina type her opinion."
Communicate understanding	• Making others aware that their contributions are understood and meaningful to group work Respondents may physically position themselves toward group members as they contribute, they may use eye contact, nod their head, take notes, offer short affirming verbal responses and/or ask clarifying questions. At later points in their work they may connect their current thinking with past contributions using language like, "Well, like Emily was saying . . ." or "I agree with Fernanda . . ."
Encourage critique	• Encouraging lines of inquiry and thought to move beyond the personal Respondents might invite participants to reflect on their own actions. They might use language like, "Amber, you said . . . earlier, and that doesn't make sense with what you're saying now. What do you think? What is your position?"

FIGURE 6–6. Response practices

but they should also be encouraged to suggest other scenarios of how the activity might play out.

For example, if students are predominantly asking dead-end, yes-or-no questions like "Did you like this book?" teaching could be angled toward other possible responses associated with particular questions. Distribute this brief list of questions and ask students to talk in small groups about how they might respond to them:

- Did you like Aliki's book?
- How, at our school, do we help new language learners join the community?
- What are other people's experiences with language learning?
- Should students in the United States be expected to know more than one language?
- Why do people move or immigrate?

After five minutes or so, talk about which questions generated the most significant responses and/or discussion. Ask students to rate the questions in terms of which questions generated the best discussion. Their ratings and explanations are what matters: they might rate the first question as extremely generative if they asked follow-up questions. Highlight and add to their thinking as part of your teaching. If students say no one in their group could think of what your school is doing to help new language learners, think aloud questions that will take conversations in different yet related directions: *Why don't we know about what our school is doing? What if our school isn't doing anything?* Comparing how various groups responded to the same questions helps students discover the role of generative, open-ended questions and see that there are many ways of engaging with a question, line of inquiry, and/or invitation.

Playing out various scenarios also prompts students to think about when and how particular types of questions come into play. A strategy lesson could begin with a question like "When might process questions be needed and how might they be used?" Then, as a class or in small groups, students could come up with various scenarios, along with the accompanying actions. Be sure to take the time to imagine together what these related actions are. Preparing a chart in shared writing is one option. Asking groups of students to role-play the situations is another. The important thing is that students need to develop a clear image of the possibilities.

Scenario planning also involves thinking out possible responses to or directions for a particular question or line of inquiry. It may help to guide students to think aloud about possible actions. For example, look at the questions in Figure 6–7 and consider the possible scenarios generated beneath each one. Talking through these options and inviting students to suggest additional options will help them develop wider images of what might be possible when they work on future invitations.

Purpose for attending to process	To start group activity	To refocus group work	To find a stopping point	To begin work again with the same group on a different day
Question	"What should we do?"	"How is that related to what we're doing?"	"How can we do this during invitation time?"	"What are we going to do now?"
Possible scenario	Group members could first look through the whole folder and see what interests them. They could list options for starting and then rate them as a group. They could start with their first choice and return to other suggestions if needed and if interests continue.	Responding to a question like this could lead a group member to explain the connection they're making between a suggestions/topic/or story and the group's work. It might also lead group members to discover unrelated work that isn't necessarily productive.	When a group decides to engage with work that they think will take a long time, they might look at the clock and determine if their agenda can be broken into parts that can be worked on over several work periods. They could estimate logical stopping points.	If a group had taken notes during their previous session and/or created memorable artifacts, they could begin with reviewing together what they had accomplished in the name of reengaging with their work.

FIGURE 6–7. Scenario planning chart

Learning from Experience

Over time, through the support of experiences like observing, mapping, sorting, and imagining scenarios, you can help students see what is possible, that while some practices are context-specific, many can be carried over from invitation to invitation. Slowing down, attending to processes, and recording and reviewing observations together encourages students to offer suggestions for next moves, augment their invitations work, and develop habits of mind that promote more effective, powerful literacy in and beyond the classroom.

The following strategy lessons are just a few among the many that will help students become skilled inquirers:

- How to initiate inquiry work and invitations activity
- How to use texts during an invitation
- How to generate questions
- How to use questions during group inquiry
- How multiple ways of knowing that can be used in pursuing an invitation
- How multiple languages that are used in inquiry
- How to keep activity focused
- How to share responsibilities
- How to keep a line of inquiry going over several weeks
- How different scenarios play out from a single invitation
- How processes and practices are made public

Invitation for All

Selecting, Focusing, and Reflecting on Teaching

Review all you know about your students. What invitation processes and practices do you want them to know more about? Choose a teaching concern that is currently on your mind. Break it down so that your teaching is focused and builds on what students already know. How might you begin this teaching—observing, mapping, sorting, imagining scenarios? Remember that good teaching, along with time and experience, leads students to take on new practices. Watch closely as your students attempt to use the strategies you've taught them. What do their approximations teach you about your next teaching moves?

Teaching in the Moment

7

Fishbowls, maps, and charts are all ways to help children think about what they might do when working on an invitation. Teaching these strategies in minilessons addresses many children's needs and supports inquiry in many different contexts. These lessons help students develop holistic images of what it's like to think and act as critical inquirers. But sometimes needs are specific to an individual, a group, or a specific line of inquiry. Students may need help working through specific issues and/or fine-tuning practices in the midst of their invitation work. This kind of teaching takes place in the moment.

Teaching in the moment means we might stop by and help students become explicitly aware of the moves they're making. We might help students name current dilemmas with the hope of helping them identify possible next steps. We might offer advice to groups regarding new options for problem posing and/or problem solving. We might join a group as a co-learner, collaborating in genuine inquiry with the other members. As teachers and students interact, who is teaching and who is learning constantly shift. Just as we can be learners, students can be teachers. When students point out useful strategies, suggest options for furthering their group's work, or demonstrate possible ways of inquiring, they are teaching.

In-the-moment teaching, like minilessons, is driven by what participants need most at the time. Identifying needs takes time. When approaching students at work, taking time to observe carefully and get a sense of what students are doing before jumping in is key. Remember, observing is teaching too—it's a way of telling students their processes are valuable and that we're interested in seeing how they put into action all that they currently know. Then, based on what we see, we can decide how (and if) intervention will develop what the students currently know about being a critical inquirer.

At times we may decide not to interrupt the flow and instead make a note or two about a particular aspect of a group's work to discuss with them later. At other times, based on our observations and interpretations, we may decide that pausing a group's work is beneficial.

Once a focus for teaching has been selected, the question becomes, *how* do I teach it? Whether we stop by, join an invitation from the start, or interact with invitation participants during their minipresentations, we can teach by:

- Naming what students are currently doing.
- Offering advice to help move the group or individual inquirers forward.
- Demonstrating new inquiry practices.

The classroom examples that follow are not meant to imply that teachers and learners must interact in only these ways; rather, my point is that language matters. As teachers, we need to attend to how we interact with students. Our teaching moves need to be clear and precise. Teaching interactions need to include space for students to either confirm or challenge that teaching. Good teaching welcomes honest response and must be revised when students respond in unexpected ways. We need to be open-minded, carefully reexamining our teaching moves and language to see how we can improve the clarity of our intentions or shift our focus to match student needs. Therefore, think flexibly about these suggestions. Consider how they would look, sound, and feel like in your teaching.

Naming

Names come from experience. When we encounter a roadblock, see people seated along the sidewalks, and hear a marching band approaching, we know we're about to see a parade. When we hear two people having a loud, rapid, overlapping, heated debate, we might say they're having an argument. Our students, depending on their experiences, might share this understanding of what constitutes a parade or an argument, but can they identify practices like negotiation, code switching, thinking aloud, and critique in similar ways? They may "know" some of these words but not have an image of what these practices look like in action or what it might mean to undertake such practices themselves. Naming practices in the moment can help students become aware of what they are doing and be able to use these practices elsewhere in their learning lives.

Teaching grounded in kidwatching calls us to shift back and forth between attending to what students are doing and interpreting these actions in terms of what they currently understand. These interpretations then inform our teaching. Pulling up a chair and spending five or ten minutes with a group can reveal a great deal about children's understanding of literacy and inquiry.

Let's go back to the Memories invitation featured in Chapter 6. After Nina, Shelly, and Ana Cristina finish their futból/football/soccer discussion, Shelly goes back to reading from *Marianthe's Story: Painted Words, Spoken Memories*. Notice what the students do, as well as the ways to interpret and name their current understanding about invitations and inquiry practices.

What happens as students inquire together

What students appear to understand about invitations and inquiry practices

When Shelly finishes reading a page, she turns to Ana Cristina and passes her the book, looking at her all the while. Despite Ana Cristina's initial hesitations, she begins to read,

- Communicating with others involves reading body language and gestures.
- Recalling earlier interactions informs present actions. (Shelly remembers Ana Cristina's initial physical distancing of herself from the group and interprets this as being hesitant to participate.)
- Expecting that all group members take risks and participate, Shelly uses her gaze to support, encourage, and communicate this expectation to Ana Cristina.

"'She went straight to an easel and began to paint.' Oh, pintando pinturas [pointing to the picture]. 'Mari is an artist.'" Ana Cristina continues, alternating her attention between the printed text and illustrations and offering side commentary in Spanish ("Ella se siente triste" when she looks at the illustration of Mari looking sad in front of the picture she has painted of her family).

- Using one's first language when thinking aloud supports comprehension.
- Attending to illustrations in addition to words furthers possible understanding.

As the girls finish reading, Shelly returns to a passage that compares printed English text to chicken's feet and camel humps. She turns to Ana Cristina and Nina and asks, "Was it like that for you?" Shelly seems surprised as she listens to the similarities between her classmates' experiences and those of the main character in the book.

- Learning from classmates' lived experiences makes stories "real" and worthy of contemplation.

Nina explains, "When I found out we coming to Newtown, knew a few letter and my name. R, A, B, and name." Listening, Ana Cristina nods in agreement as she walks to the art cupboard to get paints. Shelly follows up with, "So, I wonder why this author wrote this book. Maybe she wanted others to know the hard parts about immigrating. It's not just moving." Then the girls, like the character Marianthe, decide to paint.

- Communicating includes interpreting body movements and gestures.
- Making public connections between texts and lives furthers group thinking.
- Painting is one option for constructing and communicating meaning.

Watching this group at work reveals many useful practices. Combining what we've just seen with what we may know from other contexts often helps narrow our in-the-moment options. As with minilessons, we don't want to teach everything at once. Brief interactions facilitate focused reflections, help students hang on to teaching, and allow participants to return to work.

Because Ana Cristina is often a reluctant participant who has taken the risk to read in the company of others, her teacher might decide to highlight an aspect of her work: thinking aloud in another language. She could begin by asking, "Do you know what I just observed Ana Cristina do as she was reading?" If the group can't reconstruct Ana Cristina's actions in detail, she might "rewind," using her notes to retell what she observed. "She took the book from Shelly, read a line of text in English, pointed to the pictures, said something in Spanish, and then resumed reading. Why might she have done this? And why might this have been a smart move on her part?"

Together, the teacher and the three girls can now tease out how Ana Cristina used her first language to think aloud during her reading so that she could make sense of text. The teacher might also point out that no one else in the group or the class is a Spanish speaker and that a primary purpose of Ana Cristina's talk is to further her own understanding of the text. As this reflective conversation comes to a close, the teacher can then name what transpired, using the same language she used in the conversation: "Thinking aloud or in your head in another language as you read in English can help you make sense of what you're reading."

Stopping the girls' work to illustrate how a first language can be used during learning not only is substantive feedback about what Ana Cristina has done but also invites Ana Cristina and Nina to use their first languages in the future. Naming what Ana Cristina is doing also helps Shelly recognize the work that is unfolding as learners problem-solve their way through a new language.

There are other naming options the teacher could focus on based on this same interaction:

- Ways children use their bodies to communicate
- How reading takes place (reading aloud, shared reading, silent reading)
- Ways in which group members share responsibilities (and how this is different from everyone taking a turn at the same thing)
- How illustrations can support meaning
- Ways in which children can learn from one another's lives
- What making connections sounds like
- Ways in which learners can use multiple ways of knowing to think through issues as well as share their thinking with others

The list could go on. The point is that the girls seem to be doing many of the things on this list, but they may or may not be aware of their moves. Naming what group members do helps children think explicitly about their practice. When they know and can talk about what they're doing, they increase the number of options they can intentionally draw on in the future when they encounter difficulty.

Offering Advice

Advice permeates our everyday lives: we call family members when we hit a cooking or cleaning snag, discuss a personal dilemma with friends over coffee, or ask colleagues for professional tips. Sometimes, too, advice is offered without solicitation. Either way, it is usually most successful when it is shared between trusting, credible people: we hold on tighter to cooking advice from experienced chefs and gardening suggestions from active gardeners. For advice to thrive in the classroom, students need to trust one another and see their classmates, as well as their teachers, as credible members of their inquiry community. In other words, if a teacher shares advice based on strategies he uses when engaged in inquiry, students need to see and trust him as a fellow inquirer. As experienced inquirers discuss how they have approached invitation work, worked through problems, and negotiated practices, they not only help others use similar strategies, ways of thinking, processes, and practices but also strengthen what they know about their own learning practices.

Asking Critical Questions

The Memories group used several languages, visual images (illustrations and paintings), and body movement to construct and communicate meaning. During their minipresentation on immigration, they told their classmates that Nina and Ana Cristina had experienced confusions and difficulties similar to those the character Marianthe had in *Painted Words, Spoken Memories*. They also showed their own paintings and asked classmates to interpret what they'd painted.

Their presentation leaned heavily on what they did. If their teacher wanted to encourage a more critically engaging presentation, she might share what she would do if she were a participant in the group:

> Sometimes when I'm surprised by something, I'm interested in others' thinking or experiences. Shelly, if I were you, I might take what I learned from the book and from Nina and Ana Cristina and use my thinking to invite others to rethink what they know about language learning. For example, during your presentation you might pose a question to the class instead of retelling what your group did. Based on what this group shared about their work today, what are some possible questions?

Classmates might then suggest questions like these: "What do you think are challenges for people learning new languages?" "When people say things like 'just learn English,' what might they know (or not know) about language learning?"

Using Multiple Ways of Knowing

Using multiple ways of knowing often leads to better communication and deeper understanding. Therefore, we may decide to encourage our students to think about how language, art, music, math, drama, and movement can be used as learning tools and how ways of knowing influence what one comes to know, communicate, and question.

For example, their teacher might extend the Memories group's presentation by posing a question to the class ("What did you notice about how Nina, Ana Cristina, and Shelly used painting in their work?") or to the group participants ("What meaning-making tools did your group draw on as you worked today?"). Building on the responses she receives, her advice might sound something like this:

> As I'm learning, I often think about how I can best express what it is that I'm thinking. Sometimes that means painting, as these girls did. Sometimes it means using many ways of knowing at the same time, as Ana Cristina did when she added words to her painting or as Nina did when she told stories about life in Israel as she painted. As I work, I keep in mind what happens when I create a sculpture or a painting or a poem. I don't set out to create a masterpiece; rather, I'm using shape, form, color, or language to help further what I know and think. The next time you're working, you might explore how art, movement, math, language, drama, and music help you construct and communicate different meanings. Pay attention to what happens when you use many ways of knowing to help you think.

When we're offering advice, we're sharing what experienced inquirers might do if they were participants in a given situation. Wrapping up that advice with "you could try this too" helps bridge our suggestions to our students' future actions. Inviting students to make their experiences visible reiterates the value of ongoing processes—what we talk about today is important tomorrow and the next day.

Talking with and Back to Texts

Advice can also center on using a specific strategy. Watching a group navigate a difficult text with limited success, we might "pause" their work and suggest they use a particular strategy—talking with and back to the text by writing in the margin. For example, a group working on a Human Rights invitation had printed an Internet article that contained a lot of official-sounding jargon. Their teacher's advice to this group might sound something like this:

> I've been watching you read this article, and it sounds difficult to understand. One thing I do when I'm trying to work through difficult material is to make notes in the margin as I read. It becomes sort of a double-entry journal, with the author's thinking in one column and my thinking in another column. I might summarize what I understand, write down questions I have about what I've read, react to what the author is saying. Then I can go back and read through my thinking to see if I can create a bigger picture about what the author is trying to say. Try this with the article you're working on and see how it works for you.

In this example, the message is stronger: "I want you to do this now," not "perhaps you could try this in the future." We constantly make decisions about what we want to do in the classroom and the words we will use to carry out those intentions. In this instance the decision was to be directive: students often don't know whether a strategy will work for them until they've tried it. Nevertheless, the advice still allows for future choice. If the students decide the double-entry journal approach doesn't work for them, they probably won't use it in the future. However, if the strategy enables them to work through the article in a meaningful way, they will no doubt continue to use it.

Demonstrating Critical Literacy Practices

When we learn to skate, jump rope, or dive, we often do so from an experienced skater, jump roper, or diver, in the company of other would-be skaters, jump ropers, or divers. The teacher gives explicit demonstrations, then practices these moves along with us as we have a go. We might watch the other students as they try to become skaters, jump ropers, or divers alongside us. The point is that we come to see what is possible. We gather tips and tools as we watch and interact. Chances are we may not immediately learn to skate backward, jump double-dutch, or dive from the high board, but we have the opportunity to watch these feats and work through how we might someday accomplish them.

The same can be said for teaching and learning critical literacy practices. If invitations address real and complex issues, chances are that simple, singular, sequential, or finite options for action won't present themselves. Therefore, paying attention to what others are doing can further what participants imagine as possible when they develop and pursue their inquiries. New options are constantly demonstrated as students work with one another. When teachers join in, they too demonstrate new possibilities.

When children are working on invitations, we often move from one group to another. We may sit on the sidelines and observe, name a process or technique, offer advice, or give a brief demonstration. Sometimes, we'll spend an entire work session with one group, gaining insights into the ebb and flow of the group's processes as well as giving ongoing, embedded demonstrations of various roles and responsibilities. Sometimes we may act as facilitator and help develop a group plan of action. At other times, our own knowledge of and experience with a topic allows us to clarify the students' current understanding. Or we may know about and suggest additional useful resources to turn to. And, since students are invited to bring their experiences and cultural resources to invitation activity, we could demonstrate how to contribute to and further group thinking by using our own lives and resources.

In the example below, a teacher is inquiring along with a group of students, learning from and with them. The group is unusually large, but the students are passionate about being part of it and are determined to make it work. The activity they undertake illustrates how both teachers and students can teach through demonstration and how an array of critical strategies, practices, and literacies can be used to inquire and take action.

Eight students in Room 4 (Jenna, Emily, Mary, Amy, Missy, Mitch, Shelly, and Sara) and their teacher gather around a table to work on an In the News invitation. Recently, the class has noticed local newspaper articles on standardized testing, AYP (annual yearly progress), and school success/failure. One headline and article in particular caught their eye: "Maplewood Elementary and Nine Other Schools Failing." This article and numerous other newspaper, magazine, and journal articles taking a variety of positions on testing, school achievement, and culture are in the invitation folder. David Smith's *If the World Were a Village* (2002) is also tucked inside.

Reading Critically

To read critically is to read words and worlds that are both present and missing. Critical readers see language as a potential object of inquiry into the relationships between literacy and power. When readers study language they examine how words, grammatical constructions, and images are used to position people in particular ways. Questioning *how* language is used and the social consequences of its use is one way of questioning "common" and often unquestioned ways of thinking about "facts" and how they come to be represented in the world (Janks 1991; Comber and Simpson 1995).

Invitation: In the News: Beyond Facts, Reading News Critically

Reporters, columnists, and advertisers (as well as all writers and makers of texts) work to convince readers to think about the world, facts, and their needs in particular ways. They want readers to walk away thinking certain things about the world and/or what they can or can't do.

Sometimes they present information as if it is *normal* or *the truth* rather than a possibility. They do this when they decide:

- who they will talk to,
- what information they will use or not use,
- what words they will use in the story,
- what pictures or images to use, and
- how they will arrange the words and images together to frame the story they're telling.

Therefore it is up to readers to read what is there and what is missing with a critical mind.

For example, when reporting on changes in affordable housing, reporters make choices. They might say, *The doors are shutting on needy renters.* Using these words in this way makes the doors responsible. If in the article they interview only the renter who is soon to be out of a home, the story seems sad and it appears like it's the renter's fault for not making enough money—not the fault of the city for high housing costs and too many low-paying jobs. The same event could be told another way. Think about the article if it started with: *The government has decided that they won't be helping needy renters anymore.* Now, with those words, members of the government are responsible. It changes the situation and who can do something about it. Maybe the government should be thinking about minimum wages and cost of living in urban areas, etc. It matters what viewpoints are shared and how news is presented.

You're invited to read any recent piece of "news." It can be classroom news, community news, and/or world news.

As you read, think about:

- What information was used to develop this story?
- What information is missing?
- What language was used?
- What images are used, not used?
- Who benefits from the story the way it is currently told?
- How else could the news be reported?

In the following transcript, the demonstrations of possible practices are highlighted.

Observations	Demonstrations of possible practices
Emily initiates the conversation, stating, "I think we could try and think about [this article]." Most group members agree and start reading and talking about standardized testing, learning at home and in school, and the diversity of schools and the world.	Invitation work can begin with suggestion. Critical inquiry connects current work with the world.
Jenna then questions the wording of the headline: "And why was only one named? They list the other names in the article but not in the headline. Or in the picture, look at this, the picture is of Maplewood Elementary students. It's almost saying Maplewood is the main one, but that's not true."	Critical reading attends to stories told and untold—and to how language is used to accomplish the telling of particular stories.
Sara asks for clarifications, which leads to a conversation about the linguistic diversity of students. Students question how test results can reflect the language learning that is occurring in schools. Some begin rereading the article.	Inquiry calls for participants to be active meaning makers who ask questions when they are unclear about something.

Mitch notes that it isn't just ENL perspectives that are missing but also the perspectives of kids at Maplewood Elementary and the other nine schools.

Missy offers her perspective as a student who lives in a household where Persian, German, and English are spoken: she knows many things that aren't included on tests.

The teacher asks, "Missy, what did you say? It was something about testing and education—"

Missy repeats her statement, and group members continue to talk about school learning, life learning, and what people need to learn. Some students peruse *If the World Were a Village* and a magazine article on the changing cultural landscapes. Sara says, "Not everyone learns the same."

The teacher says, "It seems like your comment, Sara, is related to what we're talking about here."

Emily says, "So what are we trying to do?"

Their teacher responds, "That's a useful question. Did you hear Emily? Why don't you say it again?"

Critical inquiry is about reading what is missing as well as what is present.

Invitation work invites participants to bring their experiences into inquiry—not just for sharing but for furthering thinking.

Collaborative inquiry calls participants to attend to what is being said; productive group work may require returning to statements and questions.

Collaborative inquiry allows participants to contribute and participate in diverse ways— they can be reading different texts and engaged in other kinds of related activity and be considered active participants.

Invitation work calls for practices that link many lines of thinking.

Inquiry calls for decision making and agendas.

Collaborative inquiry calls participants to attend to what is being said; productive group work may require returning to statements and questions.

Observations

Emily restates her thinking. "What are we trying to do with this invitation? We don't know. Are we trying to—" Jenna interrupts and finishes Emily's question: "—prove a point?"

As the group begins to talk about what they want to happen with this invitation, more questions emerge. "School populations changed, it said that in the article. How were school populations decided? Why were only some schools multilingual?" They make a list of their questions. Their interests seem to be gravitating toward perspectives present in and absent from the article.

Jenna suggests, "If you could talk to a person at the newspaper, what would you say?"

The teacher says, "That's an interesting point. Now you're thinking about how you could use your voice to introduce a missing point of view." After several students share what they would say, the teacher takes her turn: "So, I can tell you, I just wrote down four things I want to say, including points not in the paper. Maybe this can help you think of what you'd say—when we're on the spot, we can jot notes to help us say what we think more clearly. I want to talk about how tests are related to culture." She ends by inviting Sara's thinking, "Sara, what would you say to the paper? What do you think about all of this?"

Sara looks up from reading *If the World Were a Village*. "I'd say like, I'm mad, or something like that. I'm thinking, why are you saying something bad about schools? I heard my father talking about this with my mom in Berber. Now I ask questions."

Demonstrations of possible practices

Inquiry calls for decision making and agendas.

Critical inquiry is about generating new questions as new information is encountered as well as reading what is present and what is missing.

Critical inquiry involves talking back to texts and taking action.

Critical invitation work explores other points of views and story lines.

Inquiry involves thoughtful participation, which can sometimes be facilitated by jotting notes before articulating thinking.

Collaborative inquiry involves all members of the group, which sometimes means extending a direct invitation to participate.

Invitation work looks different for all participants—when participants are involved in seemingly peripheral activity they can still be actively engaged with the group inquiry.

Observations

Mitch suggests that maybe they can write letters. Emily suggests they present their work to the class and invite others to join in. She shows the notes she's taken on their discussion so far (see Figure 7–1). The students create an overhead inviting others to form a committee to explore the issue and take action (see Figure 7–2).

**Demonstrations
of possible practices**

Critical inquiry calls participants to take informed action via research, committee work, and text production that challenge current conditions/suggest future action.

When Jenna focuses on the wording of the headline and the choice of photograph ("And why was only one named? They list the other names in the article but not in the headline. Or in the picture, look at this, the picture is of Maplewood Elementary School students. It's almost saying Maple is the main one, but that's not true") she is examining language critically. Her classmate Mary adds to this language inquiry by wondering about the right of newspapers to construct particular stories ("Why do the papers get to decide which schools to put in the paper?"). Another classmate, Mitch, tries to explain the decision this way: "It is the law that tests scores have to become public information. They have to be released." But this isn't what Jenna and Mary are getting at. They understand that test scores may go public, but they question *how* that has been done and the power of the paper to position Maplewood Elementary in a different light than the other eight schools. Jenna and Mary feel that the paper had a hand in decisions that heightened the attention on

FIGURE 7–1. Emily's notes   FIGURE 7–2. Overhead sign-up sheet

Maplewood. These students imagine different consequences for different uses of language. They think that if the headline read "Ten Schools Failing" and no picture was used, a different story would be told.

Closely attending to language enables these critical readers to think beyond "facts and opinions" to authoring, agency, and power. Similar studies of language are possible when students juxtapose texts, read against the grain, and think about how layout and images contribute to the telling of particular versions of stories.

Engaging in Democratic Dialogue

The previous transcript has been condensed to show the wide range of demonstrations that took place. The actual discussion was much longer. The condensed version masks the ways their discussion wandered in and out of focus, the details the students explored, and exactly how this group negotiated and settled on an agenda. However, if we want to help students become critically literate citizens, they need to participate in democratic practices. Living democratically is about more than structure or procedure. Democracy is ongoing, and we create it by deliberating together and going public with our thinking. We co-author possibilities as we talk, exchange ideas, and transform one another's perspectives. Democracy is nonlinear and messy. It involves difference, respect for others as equals, and the development of social agendas. Democratic practices are communicative and fluid. We become democratic by participating in real democratic dialogues.

In the In the News invitation, group activity was initiated through fourteen exchanges in which students negotiated roles and starting points. Notice the voices present and the voices missing. Notice what the teacher doesn't do and how her decisions demonstrate that democratic practice involves dialogue and negotiation.

1. TEACHER: So I'm interested in being a part of this group.
2. MITCH: Who will all be here? Is somebody in charge? (*Emily shows him the list of participants she's written down in her notebook.*)
3. AMY: Do you guys want to vote on what we'll do or something?
4. MARY: Well nobody should really be in charge, there's lots of us here but—
5. AMY: Everybody should be in charge. But what should we do?
6. MISSY: What did people say so far? Look, Sara and Shelly were reading *If the World Were a Village*. I think it's related.
7. EMILY: I think we should read through [the book, newspaper, and magazine articles].
8. JENNA: No, I think we should like read the newspaper, that's why we're here.
9. EMILY: I think we could try to think about [this article], not just read it.

10.	JENNA:	Like you said, maybe we could talk a little about it when we read.
11.	MARY:	I already read it, so I could just tell you about it.
12.	JENNA:	Where is the article?
13.	MISSY:	Right here. Well really it's continued on page 10, too.
14.	MITCH:	It says Maplewood Elementary and nine other schools failing.

In these opening minutes, the students don't need strategies or help with practices, they need time. Given this time, they are able to negotiate and make decisions. There is tension—Mitch thinks they need a leader, Amy initially agrees and proposes voting as a way to start their work quickly, Mary challenges this assertion, and so on. Their ideas are different, and their decisions didn't lead to full consensus—Shelly and Sara keep reading *If the World Were a Village* while partially listening. Becoming critically literate involves experiencing democratic dialogue and practice. It requires knowing what it feels like to be in the midst of tension and be capable of deliberation that doesn't shut down new possibilities and lines of thought. Teaching democratic practice sometimes involves demonstrating—by not intervening—that time and experimentation are part of the process.

Choosing Language that Supports Collaborative Inquiry

Having illustrated the value of staying on the sidelines, let's consider how a teacher's demonstrations when participating in the action can help students take on language practices that support critical engagement. Democratic critical practices are about considering others' perspectives—to do so requires listening and thinking back. We can't just march forward, we have to look back, reflect, and tease through what is being shared. In this exchange, the teacher says:

- Missy, what did you say? It was something about. . . .
- It seems like your comment, Sara, is related to what we're talking about here.
- Did you hear Emily? Why don't you say it again?
- That's an interesting point. Now you're thinking about how you could use your voice to introduce a missing point of view.
- Sara, what would you say to the paper? What do you think about all of this?

This teacher is demonstrating the many ways language can slow down activity, be used to go back and contemplate, connect, or challenge what has been said. At times the teacher names what the students are doing. At other times, she invites participants to reiterate their thinking, perhaps to help them articulate a stance better or prompt them to consider someone else's thoughts. And, in her last comment, she demonstrates a way to invite quieter voices into the conversation. Sara had spent much of her time read-ing David Smith's book while listening in on the larger group's dialogue. Her contribution demonstrates that one need not talk constantly or do what the majority of the group is doing in order to participate effectively.

Introducing Other Critical Literacies

School practices often include shared reading or writing sessions, in which teachers and students collaborate to demonstrate how readers turn pages in books, how poets compose lines and stanzas, or how writers create enticing leads for their stories. Reading and writing poetry, stories, reports, and essays are common literacy practices. However, in order to live as crit-ically literate people, students need access to other literacy practices too. They need to read newspaper articles and letters to the editor, as the mem-bers of the In the News invitation group did. They need to know about petitions, press releases, and grants. And they need experiences writing talking points and composing pieces that talk back and transform current social conditions.

Counternarratives. Jenna introduced this thinking and writing genre by inviting the students collectively to compose a counternarrative to the story told in the newspaper. The students had identified that kids' voices were missing. When we discover missing voices, we can do something. In this case, the students began to compose an oral version of the story that included other voices—specifically the voices of teachers and students.

Talking points. The teacher demonstrated how writing down our thinking before speaking can help us frame our thinking clearly before going public.

Notes. Emily took notes as the group talked (see Figure 7–1). She had appropriated a frequently demonstrated practice (her teacher took notes; whenever she saw me, I was taking notes), and she demonstrated how her notes could be used to invite other class members to join in the group's efforts.

Committees. Through previous demonstrations and experiences this group of students knew that taking social action was a collective and informed effort. Lasting change isn't usually the result of individuals making spur-of-the-moment decisions. Drawing on their experiences, they assem-bled a committee.

Classrooms need to be places in which practices such as rewriting/ redesigning stories, composing talking points to articulate thinking, taking notes, forming committees, and so on, become integral practices. Our stu-dents will continue to write stories and poems if those genres are the only ones with which they're familiar. To become critically literate, they need exposure to, demonstrations of, and experiences with a wide range of possi-ble literacy practices.

INVITATIONS FOR ALL

Looking Closely at Our Moves and Ways with Words

Think about where you are in the process of inviting students to live as critical inquirers in your classroom. What is your role in the action? Get a tape recorder and blank tape. Carry it with you as you work with students. Then listen to the tape: What are you saying? What words and phrases are you are using? How are students responding? What can you say about the relationships between your contributions and the students' contributions? What is going well? Where do you see opportunities for growth?

8 Keeping Track and Moving Forward

Teaching is both a profession and an art. Learning is constructing, questioning, and reworking what we know and who we are. Teachers are learners whose curricular decisions are anchored in their assumptions about what it means to teach and learn, as well as in their images of what is possible. Wise, transformative teaching depends on agendas that are concerned with learners and the world. And such teaching begins with a current understanding of what students can do—an understanding constructed from rich, descriptive assessment.

How to collect and use everyday data to inform teaching decisions has been illustrated again and again in the classroom stories in this book. We generate data as we watch students in action and when we invite them, formally or informally, to pause, reflect, and name what they're learning. Students' notebook entries, hallway conversations, and questions also contribute to what we know about students' interests and inquiries. These data, as well as the artifacts students sometimes create, help develop our ongoing portraits of our students, their lives, and the resources they carry with them. These portraits help us identify teaching points for our strategy minilessons and in-the-moment interactions.

From this perspective toward teaching, learning, and knowing, assessment becomes ethnographic work that requires particular tools and time. It calls for experience in and techniques for gathering data in the field as members of a learning community interact. It requires the ways and means to study what is collected, searching for patterns, relationships, and needs. In the process of collecting and studying data, understanding is constructed and weighed against other data sources and participant feedback. And oftentimes understanding is revised.

In order to better understand how community members interact, pose problems, inquire, and grow as critically literate people who inquire into issues on their mind, as well as go public with their findings, new questions, and ideas for action, we, along with our students, must engage in rich, contextual ethnographic assessment practices.

Ethnographic Assessment: Sets of Potentials

There's more than one way to be an ethnographer, just as there is more than one way to assess student learning. However, ethnography and teaching share some perspectives and practices that facilitate rich understanding of people and their work. First, using a number of data sources safeguards against a simplistic understanding of the people studied. Varied sources of information lead to new understanding, insight, and action. Second, making good use of these many sources of data to inform what we know about classroom learning requires efficient and effective management systems. Fieldwork is not only collecting information: it is also knowing how to access, revisit, analyze, and use the information gathered.

Describing *how* one collects, manages, and uses data is difficult. Systems look different from person to person, classroom to classroom. The following suggestions are potential approaches to collecting and using information to support the continuous growth of teachers and students alike. Read about, consider, modify, and adapt these and other tools and strategies. Develop a system that meets your needs.

Taking Notes

Perhaps the most prevalent source of data for making curricular decisions is the interaction of learners as they inquire. We gather these data by observing and taking notes.

Carefully observing students at work takes time and experience. Setting aside time to observe is essential. As we ease into the role of ethnographer, a clock is a helpful tool. We might circulate around the room for the first five minutes of invitations work, helping out where needed, and then spend a solid fifteen minutes observing. Picking a time when kids are doing the sort of work we're interested in learning more about is important, as is communicating our commitment and purpose to the students. We might use a visual signal—clipboard, open notebook, timer—to help students remember that when we're watching groups work, we are busy and cannot be interrupted. Because we're watching to see how students work through issues, attend to dilemmas, and pursue lines of inquiry, being "unavailable" is beneficial. One, it pushes students to make decisions that they may not be used to making on their own, and two, it enables us to watch how they strategize and work out issues with peers rather than with us.

Our students may find this awkward at first. One of my favorite memories of teaching in Mexico is watching two boys inquiring into the human brain. They had constructed a large model (one they could physically fit inside) and had their other resources spread across the table. They were trying to figure out a way to simulate how information travels from nerves to the central nervous system and kept discovering reasons their ideas would not work. After about five minutes, Enrique turned to me and asked, "How should we do it?" Diego said, "She's not going to tell you." This was a good sign. While these boys were learning about the brain, they were also teasing out problems on their own, experiencing tension and drawing on their stamina. They persevered and in time devised a workable approach, with each other's help and without my intervention.

If we are working with one invitation group ourselves, we are still able to observe the other groups' minipresentations, provided these presentations include activity we are interested in knowing more about. We can also sit back and watch kids as they negotiate which invitation they will work on, decide the direction that work will take, and reflect on what they discover. Whatever our plan, we need to tell our students what we're doing and why.

As for taking notes, using a composition book for each curricular venue (invitations, writing workshop, math) works best for me. It allows me to access past notes easily and page through them as needed. But there are other options. Notes can be organized by date or student. Some teachers prefer a single notebook for all their notes (morning meeting, invitations, writing conferences, etc.), organized chronologically. Others use tabs to identify pages dedicated to individual students. Some take notes on sticky notes or labels and then file them by student.

Observation sheets can also be helpful, especially when we are paying attention to particular aspects of students' work. An observation sheet can be designed to focus on individual students, invitation groups, or the whole class. The one in Figure 8–1 helps us angle our observations toward the roles students are taking on during group activity. The chart reminds us what we've decided to attend to, and we can think specifically about the ways students' actions are contributing to the inquiry at hand. The one in Figure 8–2 focuses our thinking toward the flow of invitation activity. The one in Figure 8–3 is even more specific, focusing on how and what students are sharing during minipresentations.

Observation sheets help direct our attention to dimensions we might let slip by when taking open-ended notes. They also help organize observations of invitation activity over time, thus making changes in student activity visible. However, observation sheets can also limit to what we attend. If there isn't a box or category in which to place something students are doing, we might miss something important. Therefore, we need to design and select the sheets we use carefully: they need to meet our needs, encompass a wide range of student activity, and help us make sense of what our students are and are not yet doing.

Deciding how to take notes is step one. We then need to make another series of decisions about what and when to observe as well as what to write down. Generally speaking, observational notes are just that—observations. They might document the physical arrangement of the group, what participants do, what they say, how turns are taken, what resources and meaning-making tools are used. Notes are not a place to make judgments or interpretations.

Student's Name _____

	Invitation _____ Date _____ ____	Invitation _____ Date _____
Role Observer Participant Facilitator Leader		
Actions Comments Questions Responses Other ways of knowing		
Resources		

FIGURE 8–1. Student observation sheet

Invitation: _____

Date: _____

Group members: _____

Getting going

Pursuing inquiry

Wrapping up

Presenting thinking

Planning ahead

FIGURE 8–2. Invitation group observation sheet

Date: _____

Invitation	Group Members	*How did the invitation group share their work?* (talk, artifact[s], demonstration, discussion, illustration, diagram, media, etc.)	*What is the focus of the presentation?* (sharing new content, questions, process, etc.)

FIGURE 8–3. Minipresentation observation sheet 121

Let's look at a few examples of potential notes.

Example A

Trevor and Anthony have selected an invitation titled Agents of Change. Anthony skims the brief section of the social studies book that highlights Cesar Chavez and then begins to page through the book *Harvesting Hope.*

ANTHONY: This whole book is about Cesar Chavez, it's much longer than what is in the social studies book. We should read it. (*sets the book between them and starts to read silently*) Can I turn the page?

Example B

Trevor isn't participating in this invitation. He's not reading and Anthony is.

Example C

Anthony is doing a great job. He's interested in learning more about Cesar Chavez.

Example A paints a picture of what the boys are doing. Examples B and C are interpretations. The problem with B and C is that other interpretations are possible. Anthony may not be interested in Cesar Chavez per se but only in the differences in information between the social studies book and the picture book. Trevor may be participating but in a different way than Anthony is. We need more information about what Trevor is doing: Is he seated close enough to the book that he could be reading? Is he writing anything? If Anthony reads the whole book, how does Trevor respond? There are many possible interpretations of any event. If we record the first interpretation that comes to mind, we lose what actually happened and can no longer think about the scenario in any other, since we can't return to the sequence of events.

This is as true for the data we collect on observations sheets as it is for narrative anecdotal notes collected in notebooks. Say we're using a student-focused observation sheet like Figure 8–1. The sheet invites us to consider the roles students are taking on during their work. Just writing *facilitator* or *observer* is an interpretation. We need data to support it, as shown at the top of the following page.

Recording what Andréa said that made us think she was a facilitator lets us get a better, deeper look at her interactions over time.

While it certainly helps to see what Andréa actually said, if more notes were included about the larger context of her work with this invitation, we might change our mind about her role. Say additional notes stated that she "assigned character roles from *Seedfolks* to each group member, read the first chapter about Kim aloud, shared her comments, and then said, 'Does any-

<table>
<tr><td colspan="3">Student's Name _____Andréa_____</td></tr>
<tr>
<td>

Role
Observer
Participant
Facilitator
Leader</td>
<td>*Invitation* <u>Seedfolks</u>
(Fleishman 1999)

Date 10/04/02

Facilitator

"Does anyone have
anything else to say about
Kim?"

"Let's go on to Maricela."</td>
<td>*Invitation* _____

Date _____</td>
</tr>
</table>

one have anything else to say about Kim?'" Her role now might better be described as leader, in the sense that her comments were directive (leading the group toward her agenda) instead of moving a shared agenda forward.

Whether we use notebooks, sticky notes, or observation sheets, we must do more than just collect notes. Notes are not just archives but information for continued curricular work and action. Therefore, we must keep our notes in accessible places so that they can be returned to, reread, and used to help us understand what is happening in our classroom. Also, we need to keep our systems of evaluation consistent so that we have a frame of reference for noting growth, surprises, patterns, and/or persistent dilemmas. It takes experience to figure out what works; be sure to commit enough time to trying out a strategy before deciding whether it is or isn't working.

Replaying Activity

At the end of Chapter 7, I suggest that we can tape-record our interactions with students as a way of looking closely at our moves as well those of our students. This generative, useful practice can serve other purposes too. Say on a given day we really want to be with two invitation groups—we might position the two groups in work areas near each other so we can sit on the edge of each group. Then again, this could split our attention so that we are not able to attend closely to either group. Audio- or videotaping one group and watching the other group in person is a possible solution. At a later time we can listen to or watch the taped group's work, either on our own or with our students. Recorded data can be a helpful check on our developing skills as note takers if we use it along with live observation. Recordings let us take a second look at what we've written as we compare it with what we hear or see on the tape.

Surveying Students

There are times when we want data that speak directly to questions on our mind. Sharing these questions with our students and gathering their responses can be very useful. Say we want to know whether our students find the invitations available for them to work on pertinent to the issues with which they're currently grappling. We could create a brief questionnaire asking for student feedback on current invitations and future options (see Figure 8–4). Or we could create a survey like the one in Figure 8–5, which lists potential invitation ideas based on other data sources and proposes revisiting past invitations. If we want more than lists of ideas, we could have students write letters about what invitations they currently see as potentially engaging and what issues or themes they might like to see as invitations in the future.

Surveys can also ask students what they think is going well with invitations and how they think invitations could be more productive. This information can trigger important revisions, of course, but the fact of gathering it also demonstrates that student perspectives and contributions matter.

Tracking Activity

Students should always be part of the assessment process. There are many ways they can participate; one is by tracking their invitations work over time. An invitations activity record (see Figure 8–6) attached to students' learning logs or folders allows them to record each session's work and group members. They can also file their reflection sheets in the learning folder each week. As teachers we can then peruse student folders with a specific question in mind—for example, "What do students' lines of inquiry look like when students return to an invitation several times?" Or we might be interested in social dynamics and trace the working relationships of particular students. Or we might want to look at all the reflections of the members of a given group. Also, students can periodically review their own activity, search for patterns or relationships, describe their growth, or articulate goals for themselves or their group as inquirers and invitation participants.

Evaluating Growth, Developing Goals

When we evaluate, we identify what is desired and important within a practice. Invitations do not call students to proceed down one linear road. Therefore a single, neat continuum is not appropriate for marking and/or measuring growth. Rather, growth must be imagined in terms of a number of expanding, widening, sometimes converging and overlapping, never-ending paths as students learn from and about working with others, learn to develop and pursue agendas, learn to research multiple viewpoints, learn to listen to others, learn to rethink their previous positions, learn to envision different

Invitations Interest Survey

Name _____ Date _____

What invitations do you like most? Why?

What invitations do you like least? Why?

What themes or issues would you like to pursue with an invitation?

FIGURE 8–4. Invitation interest survey sheet **125**

Name _____ Date _____

Upcoming Invitations Survey

Would you be interested in adding any of the following invitations to the current set of options on the sign-up board? Please use numbers to show your level of interest (1 indicates the invitation you're most interested in). If you're not interested in some of the options, leave the line blank. If you have suggestions, please list them at the end.

_____ *Seedfolks: Multiple Perspectives on Community Change.* Use Paul Fleishmann's book *Seedfolks* (1999) to take on character perspectives to debate community issues.

_____ *Where in the World? Making Connections Between the Clothes We Wear and the Global Economy.* Survey where clothes are made, who makes them, and what purchasing habits mean in the larger world.

_____ *Child Labor: Is It a Thing of the Past?* You might have heard about kids working in factories during the Industrial Revolution, but are children still working? Explore various perspectives on kids and work in recent times.

_____ *Campaigns, Elections, and Government: Who Participates and How Does It Work?* Explore what it has looked like (past) and looks like (present) to live in a democracy by investigating campaigns, elections, and government through the eyes of African Americans, women, elected officials, citizens, and others.

_____ *Immigration: What Are the Issues?* You probably know something about early immigrants coming to what is now the United States, but what about the journey and lives of those who still enter the country daily? What are their stories? What issues do they face?

_____ *Great Artists: Words Tell Stories, and So Does Art.* What stories do artists tell? What issues do they take up? What do they see as their work?

_____ *Song and Social Action.* Sarah McLachlan wrote *World on Fire* and launched a campaign to make world needs visible. What issues are we, as a global community currently faced with? What is being done? What needs to be done?

_____ Other suggestions:

_____

_____

FIGURE 8–5. Upcoming invitations survey sheet

Invitations Activity Record

Name _____

Date	Invitation	Group Members

Figure 8–6. Invitations activity record

futures, and so on. There are many ways we can tackle the complexity of evaluation—revisit data, choose a focus, use flexible systems, and invite multiple perspectives into evaluation and growth conversations.

Revisiting Data

Taking time to go back helps us move forward. As teachers we need to set aside time in our routines and schedules to look at student activity and growth. Waiting until "we have some time" to review our notes is rarely successful, because the responsibilities teachers embrace are many and spare time is rarely a part of a teaching life. Review time needs to be scheduled along with everything else. Perhaps each morning when we first come to school, we can spend the first fifteen minutes reviewing data related to an invitation group or study the progress of two kids. Or we might set aside two of our preparation periods each week for reviewing our students' invitation activity. Once we establish a rhythm of returning to data and thinking through what students are doing and where they're going, these practices will become part of who we are as teachers.

Choosing a Focus

Let's say we want to know more about how students participate in invitation activity. If we're at a point when we can collect new data, we might create an observation or analysis sheet to help guide our inquiry. (An observation sheet becomes an analysis sheet when we comb back through our anecdotal notes to see what we already know about student participation.)

Look at the example in Figure 8–7. Using this format to sort through Ana Cristina's actions reveals that she is finding new ways to communicate and participate. Early in the year, she preferred ways of knowing other than spoken or written English. She used drawing, Spanish, and small-group forums to make her thinking known. In later invitations she used her Spanish to make sense of English text for herself, and in March she helped others see the links between languages as she drew on her Spanish to discover the meaning of an English word. Laying out Ana Cristina's actions over time allows us to see the ways in which she's expanding her horizons. This sheet can be used to confer with Ana Cristina, develop and articulate next steps for her, and focus our attention as we continue working with her. (A blank version of this form is included in Figure 8–8.)

Using Flexible Systems: Narratives, Observations Sheets, and Locally Generated Criteria

Data systems often require that we devise our own tools to fit specific contexts. We can start by listing descriptors aligned with what our students are currently doing or practices we intend to help students take on or by asking our students to generate lists of practices that will help them improve their invitations and inquiry work. From these lists we can create observation

Invitation Participation

Name Ana Cristina

Invitation title: __My Map Book__ Date __10/4__
Invitation title: __Memories__ Date __12/5__
Invitation title: __Why Is Learning English Hard?__ Date __3/14__

	Individual	One on One (student to student or student to teacher)	Small Group	Whole Class
Ways of Knowing and Participating Language • Written • Talk (language, shared experience, how-to explanation, planning, expression of feelings, questions/responses) Art Drama Movement Math Music	10/4 Created a map of her Mexico neighborhood by drawing and labeling in Spanish 12/5 Painted stargazing picture and wrote first English text on her own	3/14 Read *The King Who Rained* with Shelia	10/4 Ana C looked on as other group members page through *My Map Book* 12/5 Took turn reading, thought aloud in Spanish as she read in English	10/4 Pointed to locations on map as she presented 12/5 Used writing (whiteboard) and speaking in English and Spanish to present
Inquiry Roles Questions Response Resources Organizing Thinking Presenting			3/14 Worked with Fernanda to respond to Nina's questions about how to label royal family tree in Spanish (princesa, principe, rey, reina); when the group wondered what *reign* meant, Ana C noticed the similarity to *reina* and said, "Nada mas pone un g entre la I y el N"	10/4 Stood with group during presentation; responded to group questions with Adam's help to list 4 things on her map 3/14 Presented findings about Spanish/English language connections
Other notes	10/4 Placed U.S. classmate's house in Mexico neighborhood			

FIGURE 8–7. Invitation participation observation and analysis sheet

129

Invitation Participation

Name _____

Invitation title: _____ Date _____

Invitation title: _____ Date _____

Invitation title: _____ Date _____

	Individual	One on One (student to student or student to teacher)	Small Group	Whole Class
Ways of Knowing and Participating Language • Written • Talk (language, shared experience, how-to explanation, planning, expression of feelings, questions/responses) Art Drama Movement Math Music				
Inquiry Roles Questions Response Resources Organizing Thinking Presenting				
Other notes				

FIGURE 8–8. Invitation participation observation sheet

sheets, surveys, checklists, and so forth, that will help us see and record activity and growth over time.

Gathering Many Perspectives

We don't have to assess and evaluate growth on our own. If we're lucky enough to have other adults in the classroom, collaborative assessment and evaluation can generate rich thinking and discussion, as long as it's anchored in what students can do and what can be done to help them take on practices they are not yet demonstrating on their own. Invitations are a welcoming, language-rich forum in which ENL teachers and support staff can be part of the learning community. Together with classroom teachers they can observe students in action, become co-participants, and support all students as they use and learn about language in minilessons and in the-moment teaching interactions. Then, based on these experiences, everyone can collaborate to construct shared records of growth and plans for future teaching.

We can also turn to our students. Some people are quick to say that self-evaluation doesn't work. However, self-evaluation, like anything else one learns, requires experience. When my first, second, and third graders first started evaluating their own writing notebooks (both at home and in school), they often found more areas for growth than I would have pointed out or suggested. Over time, their findings, as well as the ways they articulated support for their thinking, became quite sophisticated. We need to give students consistent opportunities to step back and look at what they are learning—not grade themselves but look at their learning. We also need to be open-minded—self-evaluation isn't a guessing game in which students have to arrive at their teacher's evaluation but a critical look at self and the role of self in the larger invitation-working community. And as teachers, we need to really listen to what students are saying.

Whether self-evaluation is written or takes place in conferences or group discussions, it often helps first to describe activities without naming what we value or making suggestions for further growth. To facilitate self-evaluation, we might ask students to consider questions like these:

- What happened in your invitation group today? (They can record their impressions individually or as a group.)
- Reread what happened. What do you notice?
- What went well?
- What was the most difficult part of your work?
- What suggestions do you have for your (or your group's) next steps?

Next steps are goals. If student write or state goals, we need to find ways to ensure that these goals are at the forefront of student thinking as they launch into their next line of work. For example, we could ask students to write their next steps inside their invitation folder or learning log and reread them at the start of the next work period.

INVITATION FOR ALL

Studying Activity, Making Decisions, and Learning Together
You're invited to begin taking action in your classroom. Identify some issues
and ideas that are on your mind. Then select one student. Confer with him.
What does he notice about his work, activity, and growth? What do you
notice? Articulate some potential next steps together. Decide how both of
you will monitor and keep track of progress. Follow up with the student and
together examine data (notes, observation sheets, recordings, artifacts, etc.)
for markers of growth.

Conclusion

Inviting the World into Your Classroom

Literacy is more than mastering a list of sequenced skills, it is becoming a certain sort of person. The students you've met in this book took up invitations as curricular opportunities to engage with each other and the world. For them, becoming literate included asking questions, developing agendas, exploring perspectives, going public with their thinking, generating new questions, and working to challenge a simple understanding of the world. As these students worked with others, they took the risk of sharing their "first-draft" thinking—thinking that was sometimes challenged and later revised. As they worked with invitations and reflected on their processes, they approximated conceptual understanding and language conventions. They understood that invitations did not require them to achieve the precise understanding of a practicing meteorologist or economist or demand correctly spelled notes or conventionally edited reflections. Invitations called them to use language to learn at the same time that they were learning language. They were able to focus on making meaning in the company of their peers. When called on to communicate with others in more formal ways (a letter to the editor, a note to the principal, an article in the classroom newspaper, a poster in the school hallway), they drew on their ability to revise and edit to craft public documents using conventions that helped them be heard. Invitations ask participants to move beyond their personal life into the world—to develop practices associated with living as a critically literate person

This book provides images of and strategies for inviting students to be learners who are critically literate citizens of the world, who:

- Are passionate and open-minded, recognize the role of tension in learning, and value sustained engagement to develop new understanding;
- Are not just readers and writers but thinkers, who have access to issues and resources worth thinking about and with;
- See the complexity of their responsibilities and try to make sense of their own lives as well as the lives of others; and
- Not only are interested in and understand issues but also respond and take informed action.

Creating spaces in which students can learn to live in these ways is a big project, but one that is engaging and worthwhile. It calls for teachers and students to be risk takers and begins with trust—trust that all students can learn, trust that all students have something to say, and trust that as teachers our everyday work is helping to create the world in which we want to live.

Invitations are inquiries that matter. Participants are able to use literacy in real, genuine, and powerful ways. Invitations alter our teaching because we never know what we too will learn when we come to work each day. It takes courage and educational imagination to experiment and explore. Reinventing teaching and learning in our classrooms is social action. It is reinventing the world. And it does make a difference.

Remember Naomi Shihab Nye's words that open this book? Remember her references to the quiet minutes hidden between the noisy minutes in our busy, complex world? Keep her words, the voices of the students in this book, and the curricular possibilities invitations offer with you as you take time to find the quiet minutes to contemplate where you are, where you've been, and where you're going. Return to her words and to this book as you invite the world into your classroom and create invitations that engage students in important, critical literacy work. Together, critically literate people can imagine and create a better world.

References

Ackerman, K. 1992. *Song and Dance Man*. Illus. by S. Gammell. New York: Dragonfly Books.

Ada, A. F. 2004. *I Love Saturdays y domingos*. Illus. by E. Savadier. New York: Simon & Schuster.

Aliki. 1998. *Marianthe's Story: Painted Words, Spoken Memories*. New York: Greenwillow.

Alvarez, J. 2002. *How Tía Lola Came to (Visit) Stay*. New York: Random House Children's Books.

———. 1999. *Something to Declare*. New York: Plume.

Anderson, G. L., and P. Irvine. 1993. "Informing Critical Literacy with Ethnography." In *Critical Literacy, Politics, Praxis, and the Postmodern*, edited by C. Lankshear and P. L. McLaren. Albany: State University of New York Press.

Anzaldua, G. 1995. *Amigos del otro lado/Friends from the Other Side*. Illus. by C. Mendez. San Francisco: Children's Book Press.

Armento, B., G. Nash, C. Salter, and K. Wixson. 1994. *America Will Be*. Boston: Houghton Mifflin.

———. 1991. *A More Perfect Union*. Boston: Houghton Mifflin.

Au, K. 2001. Culturally responsive instruction as a dimension of new literacies. *Reading Online* 5(1). www.readingonline.org/newliteracies/lit_index.asp?HREF=/newliteracies/xu/index.html.

Berenstain, S., and J. Berenstain. 1981. *The Berenstain Bears and the Sitter*. New York: Random House.

Berry, J. R. 1999. *Isn't My Name Magical? Sister and Brother Poems*. Illus. by S. Hehenberger. New York: Simon & Schuster.

Bishop, R. S. 1997. Foreword to *Reading Across Cultures: Teaching Literature in a Diverse Society*, by T. Rogers and A. O. Soter. New York: Teachers College Press.

Bomer, R., and K. Bomer. 2001. *For a Better World: Reading and Writing for Social Action*. Portsmouth, NH: Heinemann.

Boozer, M. E., L. B. Maras, and B. Brummett. 1999. "Exchanging Ideas and Changing Positions: The Importance of Conversation to Holistic, Critical Endeavors." In *Making Justice Our Project*, edited by C. Edelsky. Urbana, IL: NCTE.

Brock, C. H., L. A. Parks, and D. K. Moore. 2004. "Literacy, Learning, and Language Variation: Implications for Instruction." In *Multicultural and Multilingual Literacy and Language: Contexts and Practices*, edited by F. B. Boyd and C. H. Brock with M. S. Rozendal. New York: Guilford Press.

Browne, A. 2001. *Voices in the Park*. Boston: DK Publishing.

———. 1990. *Piggybook*. New York: Dragonfly Books.

Bunting, E. 1999. *Smokey Night*. Illus. by D. Diaz. Orlando, FL: Harcourt.

———. 1998. *Going Home*. Illus. by D. Diaz. New York: HarperCollins Children's Books.

———. 1997. *A Day's Work*. Illus. by R. Himler. New York: Houghton Mifflin.

———. 1990. *The Wednesday Surprise*. Illus. D. Carrick. New York: Houghton Mifflin.

Burleigh, R. 2004. *Langston's Train Ride*. Illus. by L. Jenkins. London: Orchard Books.

Burleigh, R. 2001. *Lookin' for Bird in the Big City*. Illus. by M. Los. New York: Silver Whistle Books.

Carle, E. 1996a. *The Very Hungry Caterpillar*. Arabic edition. Translated by S. El-Nimr. London: P. Mantra.

———. 1996b. *I See a Song*. New York: Scholastic.

———. 1994. *La oruga muy hambrienta (The Very Hungry Caterpillar)*. New York: Philomel Books.

———. 1992. *La Chenille Affamee (The Very Hungry Caterpillar)*. New York: Penguin Group USA.

———. 1979. *The Very Hungry Caterpillar*. New York: Collins.

Chasnoff, D., and H. S. Cohen. 2000. *That's a Family*. Women's Educational Media. Videocassette.

Chi, M., and M. Zwonitzer, directors. 2003. *The Transcontinental Railroad*. Narrated by Michael Murphy. PBS Home Video.

Choi, Y. 2001. *The Name Jar*. New York: Random House Children's Books.

Christenbury, L. 2000. *Making the Journey: Being and Becoming a Teacher of English Language Arts*. 2d ed. Portsmouth, NH: Boynton/Cook.

Christensen, L. M. 1999. "Critical Literacy: Teaching Reading, Writing, and Outrage." In *Making Justice Our Project*, edited by C. Edelsky. Urbana, IL: NCTE.

Cisneros, S. 1997. *Hairs/Pelitos*. Illus. by T. Ybanez. New York: Random House.

————. 1991. *The House on Mango Street*. New York: Vintage Books.

Coerr, E. 1997. *Sadako*. Illus. by R. Himler. New York: Putnam.

Cohn, D. 2002. *¡Si, Se Puede!/Yes, We Can: Janitor Strike in L.A.* Illus. by F. Delgado. El Paso, TX: Cinco Puntos Press.

Collier, V. 2004. "Teaching Multilingual Children." In *Tongue-Tied: The Lives of Multilingual Children in Education*, edited by O. Santa Ana. Lanham, MD: Rowman & Littlefield.

Collins, B. 1998. *Picnic Lightning*. Pittsburgh, PA: University of Pittsburgh Press.

Comber, B. 2001. "Critical Literacies and Local Action: Teacher Knowledge and a 'New' Research Agenda." In *Negotiating Critical Literacies in Classrooms*, edited by B. Comber and A. Simpson. Mahwah, NJ: Lawrence Erlbaum.

————. 1997. "Literacy, Poverty, and Schooling: Working Against Deficit Equations." *English in Australia* 119, (20): 22–34.

Comber, B., and A. Simpson. 1995. Reading Cereal Boxes: Analyzing Everyday Texts." *Texts: The Heart of the English Curriculum*, series 1, no. 1 South Australia: Department for Education and Children's Services.

Cooke, T. 1997. *So Much*. Illus. by H. Oxenbury. Boston: Candlewick Press.

Corey, S. 2003. *Players in Pigtails*. Illus. by R. Gibbon. New York: Scholastic.

Crafton, L. K. 1981. The Reading Process as a Transactional Learning Experience. Ph.D. diss., Indiana University.

Cronin, D. 2000. *Click, Clack, Moo: Cows That Type*. Illus. by B. Lewin. New York: Simon & Schuster.

————. 2004. *Duck for President*. Illus. by B. Lewin. New York: Simon & Schuster.

Dillon, L., and D. Dillon. 2002. *Rap a Tap Tap: Here's Bojangles: Think of That!* New York: Scholastic.

Diouf, S. A. 2001. *Bintou's Braids*. Illus. by S. W. Evans. San Francisco: Chronicle.

Disney Press Staff. 2004. *Disney Princess: Volume II*. New York: Random House Disney.

Duggleby, J., and J. Lawrence. 1989. *Story Painter: The Life of Jacob Lawrence*. San Francisco: Chronicle.

Duncan, A. F., and J. G. Smith. 1996. *The National Civil Rights Museum Celebrates Everyday People*. New York: Troll Communications.

Dyson, A. H. 1999. *Social Worlds of Children Learning to Write*. New York: Teachers College Press.

Edelsky, C. 1999. "On Critical Whole Language Practice: What, Why and a Little Bit of How." In *Making Justice Our Project*, edited by C. Edelsky. Urbana, IL: NCTE.

"Emerging Mexico: A Special Issue." 1996. *National Geographic* 190 (2).

Enciso, P. E. 1997. "Negotiating the Meaning of Difference: Talking Back to Multicultural Literature." In *Reading Across Cultures: Teaching Literature in a Diverse Society,* by T. Rogers and A. O. Soter. New York: Teachers College Press.

"Mexico." 2000. *Faces* (December).

Fanelli, S. 1995. *My Map Book.* New York: HarperCollins.

Fairclough, N. 1989. *Language and Power.* New York: Longman.

Farrell, L. 1998. Reconstructing Sally: Narratives and counternarratives around work, education, and workplace restructure. A paper presented at Annual Meeting of the Australian Assoc. for Research in Education, Adelaide.

Fleishman, P. 1999. *Seedfolks.* New York: HarperTrophy.

———. 1988. *Rondo in C.* New York: Harper & Row.

Fletcher, R. 2000. *How Writers Work: Finding a Process That Works for You.* New York: HarperCollins.

Fox, M. 1991. *Wilfred Gordon McDonald Partridge.* Illus. by J. Vivas. La Jolla, CA: Kane/Miller.

———. 1989. *Feathers and Fools.* Illus. by N. Wilton. New York: Harcourt Brace.

Fraiser, M. A. 1996. *Ten Mile Day: The Building of the Transcontinental Railroad.* New York: Henry Holt.

Freeman, D. E., and Y. S. Freeman. 2000. *Teaching Reading in Multilingual Classrooms.* Portsmouth, NH: Heinemann.

Freire, P. 1972. *Pedagogy of the Oppressed.* New York: Herder & Herder.

———. 1985. *The Politics of Education.* South Hadley, MA: Bergin & Garvey.

Freire, P., and D. Macedo. 1998. *The Paulo Freire Reader.* New York: Continuum.

———. 1994. *Literacy: Reading the Word and the World.* South Hadley, MA: Bergin & Garvey.

Garza, C. L. 2000. *In My Family/En mi familia.* San Francisco: Children's Book Press.

———. 1999. *Making Magic Windows: Creating papel picado/Cut-Paper Art with Carmen Lomas Garza.* San Francisco: Children's Book Press.

Garza, C. L., H. Rohmer, and D. Schecter. 1999. *Magic Windows/Ventanas mágicas.* San Francisco: Children's Book Press.

———. 1990. *Social Linguistics and Literacies, Ideology in Disclosure.* London: Falmer.

Gee, J. P. 2004. *What Video Games Teach Us About Learning and Literacy.* New York: Palgrave Macmillan.

Gikow, L. 2003. *Be Your Own Best Friend!* New York: Golden Books, Random House.

Giroux, H. 1993. "Literacy and the Politics of Difference." In *Critical Literacy, Politics, Praxis, and the Postmodern*, edited by C. Lankshear and P. L. McLaren. Albany: State University of New York Press.

Golden Books. 2002. *Lost and Found*. New York: Golden Books, Random House.

Goodman, Y. 1985. "Kidwatching: Observing Children in the Classroom." In *Observing the Language Learner*, edited by A. Jaggar and M. T. Smith-Burke. Urbana, IL: NCTE.

Green, P. 2001. "Critical Literacy Revisited." In *Critical Literacy: A Collection of Articles from the Australian Literacy Educators' Association*," edited by H. Fehring and P. Green. Newark, DE: International Reading Association.

Greenberg, J. 2003. *Romare Bearden: Collage of Memories*. Illus. by R. Bearden. New York: Harry N. Abrams.

Grimes, N. 2002. *My Man Blue*. Illus. by J. Lagarrigue. New York: Puffin Books.

Grimes, N., G. C. Ford, and G. Ford. 1997. *Wild, Wild Hair*. Illus. by G. Ford. New York: Scholastic.

Gutierrez, K. D., P. Basquedano-Lopez, H. H. Alvarez, and M. M. Chiu. 1999. "Building a Culture of Collaboration Through Hybrid Language Practices." *Theory into Practice* 38 (2): 87–93.

Hall, M. C. 2001. *Money*. Chicago: Heinemann Library.

Halliday, M. 1978. *Language as a Social Semiotic: The Social Interpretation of Language and Meaning*. London: Edward Arnold.

Halpern, M. 2004. *Railroad Fever: Building the Transcontinental Railroad 1830–1870*. Washington, DC: National Geographic Library.

Hammell, J. 2003. "A Critical Literacy Journal." *School Talk* 8 (4).

Harrington, J. N. 2004. *Going North*. New York: Farrar, Straus, and Giroux.

Harste, J. C. 2001. "What Education as Inquiry Is and Isn't." In *Critiquing Whole Language and Classroom Inquiry*, edited by S. Boran and B. Comber. Urbana, IL: NCTE.

Harste, J. C., A. Breau, C. Leland, M. Lewison, A. Ociepka, and V. Vasquez. 2000. "Supporting Critical Conversations." In *Adventuring with Books*, edited by K. M. Pierce. Urbana, IL: NCTE.

Heath, S. B. 1983. *Ways with Words: Language, Life, and Work in Communities and Classrooms*. New York: Cambridge University Press.

Heffernan, L. 2003. "Contradictions and Possibilities." *School Talk* 8 (4).

Heffernan, L., and M. Lewison. 2003. Social Narrative Writing: (Re)constructing Kid Culture in the Writers Workshop. *Language Arts* 80 (6): 435–43.

Heide, F. P., and J. H. Gilliland. 1992. *Sami and the Time of the Troubles*. Illus. by T. Lewin. New York: Clarion.

Herron, C. 1998. *Nappy Hair*. Illus. by J. Cepeda. New York: Random House.

Hesse, K. 1999. *Just Juice*. New York: Hyperion.

Hicks, D. 2002. *Reading Lives: Working-Class Children and Literacy Learning*. New York: Teachers College Press.

Hoffman, M. 1991. *Amazing Grace*. New York: Dial Press.

hooks, b. 1999. *Happy to Be Nappy*. Illus. by C. Raschka. New York: Hyperion Books.

Hoose, P. M. 2001. *We Were There Too!: Young People in U. S. History*. New York: Farrar, Straus and Giroux.

Hughes, L. 1995. "The Negro Speaks of Rivers." In *The Collected Poems of Langston Hughes*, edited by A. Rampersad. New York: Vintage Classics.

Igus, T. 2001. *Two Mrs. Gibsons*. San Francisco: Children's Book Press.

Igus, T., and M. Wood. 1998. *I See the Rhythm*. San Francisco: Children's Book Press.

Janks, H. 2001. "Identity and Conflict in the Critical Literacy Classroom." In *Negotiating Critical Literacies in Classrooms*, edited by B. Comber and A. Simpson. Mahwah, NJ: Lawrence Erlbaum.

Janks, H. 2000. "Domination Access Diversity and Design: A Synthesis for Critical Literacy Education." *Educational Review* 52 (2), 15–30.

———. 1991. A Critical Approach to the Teaching of Language." *Educational Review* 43 (2): 191–99.

Jennings, L. B., and T. O'Keefe. 2002. Parents and Children Inquiring Together. Written Conversations about Social Justice. *Language Arts* 79 (5): 404–414.

Johnson, A. 1993. *When I Am Old with You*. Illus. by D. Soman. New York: Scholastic.

Johnston, L. 1985. *The Last Straw: A for Better or for Worse Collection*. Kansas City, MO: Andrews McMeel.

Johnston, T. 2001. *Any Small Goodness: A Novel of the Barrio*. New York: Scholastic.

———. 1996. *My Mexico—México mío*. New York: Penguin Putnam Books for Young Readers.

Jonas, A. 1987. *Reflections*. New York: Greenwillow.

Kingsolver, B. 1998. *Another America/Otra America*. Illus. by R. Cartes. Emeryville, CA: Seal Press.

Knight, M. B., and A. S. O'Brien. 1996. *Who Belongs Here?* Gardiner, ME: Tilbury House.

Krull, K. 2003. *Harvesting Hope: The Story of Cesar Chavez*. Illus. by Y. Morales. New York: Harcourt Children's.

Kuklin, S. 2002. *From Wall to Wall.* New York: Putnam Juvenile.

Kummer, P. K. 2004. *Currency.* Inventions That Shaped the World series. Toronto: Scholars Press.

Lankshear, C., and P. L. McLaren, eds. 1993. Preface to *Critical Literacy, Politics, Praxis, and the Postmodern.* New York: State University of New York Press.

Lawrence, J. 1993. *The Great Migration: An American Story.* New York: HarperCollins.

Lewinson, M., A. S. Flint, and K. Van Sluys. 2002. "Taking on Critical Literacy: The Journey of Newcomers and Novices." *Language Arts* 79 (5): 382–92.

Lewison, M., C. Leland, and J. Harste. 2000. "Not in My Classroom! The Case for Using Multiview Social Issues Books with Children." *The Australian Journal of Language and Literacy* 23 (1): 8–20.

Luke, A., and P. Freebody. 1997. "Shaping the Social Practices of Reading." In *Constructing Critical Literacies*, edited by S. Muspratt, A. Luke, and P. Freebody. Cresskill, NJ: Hampton Press.

Lyon, G. E. 1994. *Mama Is a Miner.* Illus. by P. Catalanotto. London: Orchard Books.

Madrigal, A. H. 1999. *Erandi's Braids.* Illus. by T. dePaola. New York: Putnam.

Marsh, J. 2000. "Teletubby Tales: Popular Culture in the Early Years Language and Literacy Curriculum." *Contemporary Issues in Early Childhood* 1 (2): 119–23.

McGuffee, M. 1996. *The Day the Earth Was Silent.* Illus. by E. Sullivan. Bloomington, IN: Inquiring Voices.

Medina, C. L. 2004. "Drama Wor(l)ds: Explorations of Latina/o Realistic Fiction." *Language Arts* 81 (4): 272–83.

Medina, J. 1999. *My Name Is Jorge: On Both Sides of the River.* Illus. by F. VandenBroeck. Honesdale, PA: Wordsong/Boyds Mills.

Menzel, P., C. C. Mann, and P. Kennedy. 1995. *Material World: A Global Family Portrait.* San Francisco: Sierra Club Books.

Michaels, S. 1985. "Hearing the Connections in Children's Oral and Written Discourse." *Journal of Education* 167 (1): 36–56.

Miller, W. 1999. *Richard Wright and the Library Card.* Illus. by G. R. Christie. New York: Lee and Low Books.

Moll, L. C. 2001. "The Diversity of Schooling: A Cultural-Historical Approach." In *The Best for Our Children: Critical Perspectives on Literacy for Latino Students*, edited by M. de la Luz Reyes and J. J. Halcón. New York: Teachers College Press.

Mora, P. 2001. *Love to Mama: A Tribute to Mothers.* New York: Lee and Low Books.

————. 1998. *This Big Sky.* Illus. by S. Jenkins. New York: Scholastic.

————. 1997. *Tomás and the Library Lady.* Illus. by R. Colón. New York: Random House Children's Books.

Morrison, T. 2004 *Remember: The Journey to School Integration.* New York: Houghton Mifflin.

Munsch, R. 1980. *The Paper Bag Princess.* Vancouver, BC: Annick Press.

Myers, C. 1999. *Black Cat.* New York: Scholastic.

Myers, W. D. 1996. *Brown Angels.* New York: Harper Trophy.

————. 2002. *Patrol: An American Soldier in Vietnam.* Illus. by A. Grifalconi. New York: HarperCollins.

Na, An. 2002. *A Step from Heaven.* New York: Puffin.

National Geographic Society. 1999. *National Geographic Beginner's World Atlas.* Washington, DC: National Geographic Society.

Nieto, S. 1999. *The Light in Their Eyes: Creating Multicultural Learning Communities.* New York: Teachers College Press.

Nye, N. S. 2002. *The Flag of Childhood: Poems from the Middle East.* New York: Aladdin Paperbacks.

————. 2000. *Come with Me: Poems for a Journey.* Images by D. Yaccarino. New York: Greenwillow.

————. 1996. "Newcomers in a Troubled Land." *Never in a Hurry: Essays on People and Places.* Columbia, SC: University of South Carolina Press.

O'Brien, J. 2001. "Children Reading Critically: A Local History." In *Negotiating Critical Literacies in Classrooms,* edited by B. Comber and A. Simpson. Mahwah, NJ: Lawrence Erlbaum.

Pinkney, A. D. 2002. *Ella Fitzgerald: The Tale of a Vocal Virtuoso.* Illus. by B. Pinkney. New York: Jump at the Sun/Hyperion.

Polacco, P. 1994. *Mrs. Katz and Tush.* New York: Bantam Double Day.

Popov, N. 1994. *I Dream of Peace.* New York: HarperCollins.

Ray, K. W. 1999. *Wonderous Words.* Urbana, IL: NCTE.

Recorvits, H. 2003. *My Name Is Yoon.* Illus. by G. Swiatkowska. New York: Frances Foster.

Reiner, R., and K. Gallagher. 2003. "Students Informing Our Curriculum." *School Talk* 8 (4).

Rice, E. 1993. *Benny Bakes a Cake.* New York: Greenwillow Books.

Rodríguez, L. 1998. *America Is Her Name.* Illus. by C. Vásquez. Willimantic, CT: Curbstone.

Routman, R. 1991. *Invitations: Changing as Teachers and Learners K–12.* Portsmouth, NH: Heinemann.

Rowling, J. K. 1997. *Harry Potter and the Sorcerer's Stone.* New York: Scholastic Press.

Ryan, P. M. *Becoming Naomi León*. New York: Scholastic.

———. 2002. *When Marian Sang: The True Recital of Marian Anderson.* Illus. by B. Selznick. New York: Scholastic.

Say, A. 2004. *Allison*. Boston: Houghton Mifflin.

Shange, N. 2004. *Ellington Was Not a Street*. Illus. by K. Nelson. New York: Simon & Schuster.

Shange, N., and L. Sunshine. 1999. *I Live in Music*. Illus. by R. Bearden. New York: Welcome Books.

Shannon, P. 1995. *Text, Lies and Videotape: Stories About Life, Literacy and Learning*. Portsmouth, NH: Heinemann.

Shor, I. 1987. "Educating the Educators: A Freirean Approach to the Crisis in Teacher Education." In *Freire for the Classroom, A Sourcebook for Liberatory Teaching*, edited by I. Shor. Portsmouth, NH: Boynton/Cook.

Short, K. G., and D. L. Fox. 2003. *Stories Matter: The Complexity of Cultural Authenticity in Children's Literature*. Urbana, IL: NCTE.

Short, K., Harste, J. C., and C. Burke. 1996. *Creating Classrooms for Authors and Inquirers*. 2d ed. Portsmouth, NH: Heinemann.

———. 1988. *Creating Classrooms for Authors and Inquirers*. Portsmouth, NH: Heinemann.

Shultz, C. M. 2000. *Peanuts 2000: The 50th Year of the World's Favorite Comic Strip*. New York: Balantine Books.

Smith, D. J. 2002. *If the World Were a Village: A Book About the World's People*. Toronto, ON: Kids Can Press.

Smith, F. 1998. *The Book of Learning and Forgetting*. New York: Teachers College Press.

Smith, H. A. 2003. *The Way a Door Closes*. Illus. by S. W. Evans. New York: Henry Holt.

Snow, A. 1993. *How Dogs Really Work!* New York: Little, Brown.

Tan, A. 1990. "Language of Discretion." In *State of Language*, edited by C. Ricks and L. Michaels. Berkeley: University of California Press.

Tarpley, N. A. 1998. *I Love My Hair!* Illus. by E. B. Lewis. New York: Megan Tingley Books.

Thompson, C. 1998. *Empire of Mali*. New York: Scholastic Library.

Thomson, P. 2001. *Turning on Schools: Making the Difference in Changing Times*. Sidney, NSW: Allen and Unwin.

Tran, T., and A. Phong. 2003. *Going Home, Coming Home/ Ve Nhan, Tham Que Huong*. San Francisco: Children's Book Press.

The Transcontinental Railroad. 2003. Boston: WGBH Educational Foundation. Film.

Ushida, Y. 1996. *The Bracelet*. Illus. by J. Yardly. New York: Putnam.

Vander Zee, R. 2004. *Mississippi Morning*. Illus. by F. Cooper. Grand Rapids, MI: Wm. B. Eerdmans.

Vasquez, V. 2000. "Language Stories and Critical Literacy Lessons." *Talking Points* 11 (2): 5–7.

Wegars, P. 2003. *Polly Bemis: A Chinese American Pioneer*. Cambridge, ID: Backeddy Books.

Wheeler, R. S., and R. Swords. 2004. "Codeswitching: Tools of Language and Culture Transform the Dialectally Diverse Classroom." *Language Arts* 81: 470–80.

Williams, V. B. 2004. *Amber Was Brave, Essie Was Smart*. New York: HarperCollins.

———. 1984. *A Chair for My Mother*. New York: William Morrow.

Winter, J. 2002. *Frida*. Illus. by A. Juan. New York: Scholastic.

Wolcott, K. *Be Your Own Best Friend*. Illus. by L. A. Sikow.

Woodson, J. 2002. *Our Gracie Aunt*. Illus. by J. Muth. New York: Hyperion.

———. 2000. *Miracle's Boys*. New York: J. P. Putnam's Sons.

———. 2000. *Sweet, Sweet Memory*. Illus. by F. Cooper. New York: Disney Press.

Wright, R. 1998. *Black Boy*. New York: HarperCollins.

Yarbrough, C. 1979. *Cornrows*. Illus. by C. Byard. New York: Putnam & Grosset.

Yashima, T. 1976. *Crow Boy*. New York: Puffin.

Yin, L. P. 2003. *Coolies*. Illus. by C. K. Soentpiet. New York: Puffin.

Young, K. R. 2002. *Small Worlds: Maps and Map Making*. New York: Scholastic.

Zolotow, C. 1972. *William's Doll*. Illus. by W. B. DuBois. New York: Harper Trophy.

Index